First World War
and Army of Occupation
War Diary
France, Belgium and Germany

37 DIVISION
Divisional Troops
37 Sanitary Section
31 July 1915 - 31 March 1917

WO95/2526/3

The Naval & Military Press Ltd
www.nmarchive.com
Published in association with The National Archives

Published by

The Naval & Military Press Ltd

Unit 10 Ridgewood Industrial Park,

Uckfield, East Sussex,

TN22 5QE England

Tel: +44 (0) 1825 749494

www.naval-military-press.com

www.nmarchive.com

This diary has been reprinted in facsimile from the original. Any imperfections are inevitably reproduced and the quality may fall short of modern type and cartographic standards.

© **Crown Copyright**
Images reproduced by permission of The National Archives, London, England, 2015.

Contents

Document type	Place/Title	Date From	Date To
Heading	WO95/2526/3 1915 Aug-1917 Mar 37 Sanitary Section		
Heading	37th Division Medical 37th Sanitary Section Aug 1915-1917 Mar To 5 Army		
Miscellaneous	37th Divl. Sanitary Section Vol. I August 15 Dec 16 Summarised But Not Copied		
Heading	War Diary Of 6/C Sanitary Section, 37th Division, B.E.F. From 31-7-1915 To 31-8-1915		
War Diary	Southampton	31/07/1915	31/07/1915
War Diary	Havre	01/08/1915	02/08/1915
War Diary	Tilques	03/08/1915	03/08/1915
War Diary	Renescure	04/08/1915	04/08/1915
War Diary	Caistre	05/08/1915	13/08/1915
War Diary	Westoutre	13/08/1915	16/08/1915
War Diary	Caistre	17/08/1915	26/08/1915
War Diary	Doullens	27/08/1915	31/08/1915
Heading	37 Divl. San. Section Vol II Sept 15 Summarised but not Copied		
Heading	War Diary of O/C Sanitary Section 37th Division From Sept 1st 1915 To Sept 30th 1915		
War Diary	Doullens	01/09/1915	05/09/1915
War Diary	Pas	06/09/1915	30/09/1915
Heading	37th Divl. San. Section. Vol. 3 Oct 15 Summarised but not Copied		
Heading	War Diary Of Sanitary Section, 37th Division, B.E.F. From Oct 1 1915 To Oct. 31 1915		
War Diary	Pas	01/10/1915	31/10/1915
Heading	37th Div. San. Sect. Vol 4 Nov 15 Summarised but not Copied		
Heading	War Diary Of Sanitary Section 37th Division B.E.F. From Nov 1st 1915 To Nov. 30th 1915		
War Diary	Pas	01/11/1915	30/11/1915
Heading	37th Division San. Sect. Vol. 5 December 1915 Summarised but not Copied		
Heading	War Diary Of Sanitary Section, 37th Division From Dec 1st 1915 To Dec. 31st 1915 (Volume V)		
War Diary	Pas	01/12/1915	31/12/1915
Heading	37th Divl. San. Sect. Vol. 6 Jan 1916		
Heading	War Diary Of Sanitary Section, 37th Division, B.E.F. From Jan. 1st 1916 To Jan 31st 1916 (Volume)		
War Diary	Pas	01/01/1916	31/01/1916
Heading	37th Divsl. Sanitary Section. Feb March April 1916		
Heading	Divl. 37th San. Sect. to Vol 7		
Heading	War Diary Of Sanitary Section, 37th Division, From Feb. 1st 1916 To Feb. 29th 1916 (Volume VII)		
War Diary	Pas.	01/02/1916	20/02/1916
War Diary	Bavincourt	21/02/1916	29/02/1916
Heading	War Diary Of Sanitary Section, 37th Division, B.E.F. From March 1st 1916 To March 31st 1916 (Volume VIII)		
War Diary	Bavincourt	01/03/1916	20/03/1916

War Diary	Lucheux	21/03/1916	31/03/1916
Heading	War Diary Of Sanitary Section, 37th Division From April 1st 1916 To April 30th 1916 (Volume IX)		
War Diary	Lucheux	01/04/1916	30/04/1916
Heading	War Diary Of Sanitary Section, 37th Division B.E.F. From:- June 1st 1916 To June 30th 1916 (Volume XI)		
War Diary	Bavincourt	01/06/1916	30/06/1916
Heading	War Diary Of Sanitary Section, 37th Division, From May 1st 1916 To May 31st 1916 (Volume X)		
War Diary	Lucheux	01/05/1916	03/05/1916
War Diary	Bavincourt	04/05/1916	31/05/1916
Heading	War Diary Of Sanitary Section, 37th Division, From July 1st 1916 To July 31st 1916 (Volume XII)		
War Diary	Bavincourt	01/07/1916	04/07/1916
War Diary	Pas	04/07/1916	15/07/1916
War Diary	Givenchy-Le-Noble	16/07/1916	16/07/1916
War Diary	Bryas	17/07/1916	20/07/1916
War Diary	La Comte	21/07/1916	26/07/1916
War Diary	Camblain L'Abbe	27/07/1916	31/07/1916
Heading	War Diary Of Sanitary Section 37 Division From Aug 1st 1916 To Aug 31st 1916 (Volume XIII)		
War Diary	Camblain L'Abbe	01/08/1916	14/08/1916
War Diary	Bruay	15/08/1916	31/08/1916
Heading	War Diary Of Sanitary Section, 37th Division From Sept 1st 1916 To Sept 30th 1916 (Volume XIV)		
War Diary	Bruay	01/09/1916	19/09/1916
War Diary	Boyeffles	19/09/1916	30/09/1916
Heading	War Diary Of 37th Sanitary Section, 37th Division From Oct 1st 1916 To Oct 31st 1916 (Volume XV)		
Miscellaneous	A.D.M.S. 37th Division	31/10/1916	31/10/1916
War Diary	Boyeffles	01/10/1916	18/10/1916
War Diary	Roellecourt	19/10/1916	20/10/1916
War Diary	Le Cauroy	21/10/1916	21/10/1916
War Diary	Beauval	22/10/1916	22/10/1916
War Diary	Marieux	23/10/1916	31/10/1916
Heading	War Diary Of Sanitary Section, 37th Division From Nov 1st 1916 To Nov. 30th 1916 (Volume XVI)		
War Diary	Marieux	01/11/1916	16/11/1916
War Diary	Hedauville	17/11/1916	17/11/1916
War Diary	Forceville	18/11/1916	25/11/1916
War Diary	Marieux	26/11/1916	30/11/1916
Heading	War Diary Of Sanitary Section, 37th Division From Dec 1st 1916 To Dec 31st 1916 (Volume XVII)		
War Diary	Marieux	01/12/1916	13/12/1916
War Diary	Frohen Le Grand	14/12/1916	14/12/1916
War Diary	Flers	15/12/1916	15/12/1916
War Diary	Monchy Cayau	16/12/1916	16/12/1916
War Diary	Norrentes-Fontes	17/12/1916	17/12/1916
War Diary	St Venant	18/12/1916	20/12/1916
War Diary	Lestrem	21/12/1916	31/12/1916
Heading	War Diary Of Sanitary Section, 37th Division From January 1st 1917 To January 31st 1917 Volume XVIII		
War Diary	Lestrem	01/01/1917	31/01/1917
Heading	War Diary Of Sanitary Section, 37th Division From. February 1st 1917 To February 28th 1917 (Volume XIX)		

War Diary	Lestrem	01/02/1917	13/02/1917
War Diary	Braquemont	14/02/1917	28/02/1917
Heading	War Diary Of 37th Sanitary Section 37th Division From March 1st 1917 To March 31st 1917 (Volume XX)		
War Diary	Braquemont	01/03/1917	03/03/1917
War Diary	Norrent Fontes	04/03/1917	08/03/1917
War Diary	Roellecourt	09/03/1917	31/03/1917

WO 95   2526/3

1915 Aug - 1917 Mar

37 Sanitary Section

37TH DIVISION
MEDICAL

37TH SANITARY SECTION
AUG 1915 - ~~DEC 1916~~
1917 MAR

TO 5 ARMY

37TH DIVISION
MEDICAL

S

37th Division

August 1915

121/6787

Summarised but not copied

37th Div: Sanitary Section

Vol: I

August 1, 15.
|
Dec '16

Confidential.

War Diary
of
O/C Sanitary Section,
3/7th Division, B.E.F.

from 31-7-1915   to   31-8-1915

H.G. Moss
Lieut
O/C Sanitary Section,
3/7th Division
(1st London (City of London Sanitary))

WAR DIARY

INTELLIGENCE SUMMARY.
(Erase heading not required.)

Army Form C. 2118.

Place	Date	Hour	Summary of Events and Information	Remarks and references to Appendices
SOUTHAMPTON	31-7-15	5.30 pm	Left Tidworth Stn. 12.20 pm. entrained with Section of 154th Co. R.E. 37th Division. Ample accommodation. Entraining numbered 1 Officer, 34 other ranks. Section motor lorry proceeded by road, leaving Tidworth Park Camp 7.20 am, arriving SOUTHAMPTON Docks 11.30 pm. 2 Drivers + one A/Sergt. in charge. Train arrived S. Docks Station 2.0 pm. Detrained 2.0 pm to 5.0 pm assisted unloading train and loading ships. Every attention shown to me, and every assistance given to me by Embarkation Officers. Lorry and Horse in charge of one Driver on "Anglo-Canadian", left 4.0 pm. Self and 26 other ranks on "Atalanta", left 5.30 pm.	
HAVRE	1-8-15		Conditions on ship (Atalanta) very crowded. 700 on board. Arrived Havre 3.15 am. Disembarked 7.30 am to 9.30 am. assisted unloading "Anglo-Canadian" Lorry re-negotiated by A.S.C. & sent for inspection. 10.0 Left Docks 11.30 am arrived at Camp No. 5. Reported to Camp Commandant. Allotted Tents & Received orders for entrainment at Gare des Marchandises at 8.30 am on 2-8-15. *(cont'd overleaf)*	

Army Form C. 2118

WAR DIARY
INTELLIGENCE SUMMARY.
(Erase heading not required.)

Instructions regarding War Diaries and Intelligence Summaries are contained in F. S. Regs., Part II. and the Staff Manual respectively. Title pages will be prepared in manuscript.

Place	Date	Hour	Summary of Events and Information	Remarks and references to Appendices
HAVRE	1-8-15 cont'd		Reported to A.D.M.T. HAVRE re Lorry. Received instructions for Lorry to proceed to ABBEVILLE at 7-30 a.m. and report to D.D.T.	
		4pm	think.	
HAVRE	2-8-15		7-30 a.m. Lorry proceeded dry road to ABBEVILLE. Two Drivers with Sergeant in charge. 8.30 Reported R.T.O. Gave distance, times. Left 11-30. Stopped at Bucky-M. (horn Latrines in most unhealthy condition. Plentiful supply, coffee hot water. Tubs for washing purposes. Stopped at ABBEVILLE	
		4pm	15 mins. Hot water available.	
TILQUES	3-8-15		5-0 a.m. arrived AUDRIQUE AUDRUICQ. Detrained and marched at 7.30AM with No. 39 Mobile Veterinary Unit to TILQUES arriving 10-45a.m. Personnel lined out. Reported DADMS en route, 10.30 a.m. A.D.M.S. called. Lorry not arrived. Received orders to	
		4pm	Moved RENESCURE on morrow (4-8-15)	
RENESCURE	4-8-15		Left TILQUES 2.30 p.m. Lorry reported at starting point TILQUES 3-0 p.m. All correct. Took up place in column 4-0 p.m. arrived RENESCURE 7-10 p.m.	
		4pm		

Army Form C. 2118

WAR DIARY
or
INTELLIGENCE SUMMARY

(Erase heading not required.)

Instructions regarding War Diaries and Intelligence Summaries are contained in F. S. Regs., Part II. and the Staff Manual respectively. Title pages will be prepared in manuscript.

Place	Date	Hour	Summary of Events and Information	Remarks and references to Appendices
CAISTRE	5-8-15	10.30 am	Joined in column en route for CAISTRE. 1-0pm to 2-0 pm mid-day halt. Men very fatigued with continual journeying. Pace very trying for feet. 5-0 pm arrived at CAISTRE. Reported at once to DADMS. Took up Billets. ADMS called. Billet satisfactory. Ground left in unsatisfactory condition by previous Unit. Open latrines found and dump heaps of manure containing swarms of fly maggots and pupa. Swarms of flies in and round Billets traced to manure heaps.	
CAISTRE	6-8-15	8.30	Reported to ADMS. Inspected Billets and Horse Lines used by Headquarters Units, and advised on suitable latrines, urinals and disposal of manure by incineration. This can be done on any incinerator mended an intelligent and conscientious officer is available. Advised that all civil closets be put out of bounds for Soldiers. Manure at own Billet piled into heap 3ft high, sprayed with creosol 1-160, paraffin 1-160 & 1 ft earth put on top & well trodden down	

T2134. Wt. W708—776. 500000. 4/15. Sir J. C. & S.

Army Form C. 2118.

WAR DIARY
INTELLIGENCE SUMMARY.
(Erase heading not required.)

Place	Date	Hour	Summary of Events and Information	Remarks and references to Appendices
CAISTRE	7-8-15	10.0 am	Inspected Billets and Horse Lines of Divisional Train Hqrs. Sanitation and conditions very fair. Great interest taken by Reg. M.O. Inspected Billets etc of Cyclists Co., positions sentries Sanitary arrangements in charge of detailed men and supervised by M.O. of Div Train. Conditions fair. Recommendations made. Condemned one Barn occupied by 32 N.C.O's & men as I found they were sleeping in portion of Barn partially screened off from Pig Pen. Arranged with Officer i/c for everyone to be moved into wagon sheds and bivouacs.	
CAISTRE	8-8-15	8.45	Reported to ADMS. Inspected Hqr. Billets etc. Being occupied by several small detachments of Hqr. Units, it was difficult to enforce measures of Sanitation. Made recommendations and left members of Sanitary Section to supervise.	
		9.30	Inspected Billets etc. of Yorkshire Dragoons (Div. Cavalry Unit) Sanitary measures in order. Found troops were sleeping in *(contd overleaf)*	

Army Form C. 2118.

WAR DIARY
or
INTELLIGENCE SUMMARY.
(Erase heading not required.)

Instructions regarding War Diaries and Intelligence Summaries are contained in F. S. Regs., Part II. and the Staff Manual respectively. Title pages will be prepared in manuscript.

Place	Date	Hour	Summary of Events and Information	Remarks and references to Appendices
CAISTRE	Cont'd 8-8-15		Upper part of barn, on open rafters, covered with loose straw directly above pig pens. Sent O.C. and recommended troops be moved to better billet or to bivouacs. Recommendations carried out. Detailed men of Section for duty here.	
CAISTRE	9-8-15	9.30	Reported to ADMS. Asked permission for self and party to visit Sanitary Officer (Lieut Draycott) 28th Division at Westoutre. Suggestion acted on. Made various inspections. Hypo limits and water tests at pumps, wells etc in Town	
"				
CAISTRE	10-8-15	9.10	Reported ADMS. Visited Billets etc 48th Field Ambulance at Eecke. Made recommendations to O.C. & inspected "A" Section Camp with him. Noticed Billets full of loose straw. Suggested it should be burnt & that Barns should be sprayed with 1 - 160 Cresol Solution, and no many troops be moved to bivouac.	
CAISTRE	11-8-15	8.45	Reported to ADMS. Made Tour of Divisional Area and ascertained positions of different units etc Eecke, St Sylvestre Cappel, St Mary Cappel (cont'd overleaf)	

WAR DIARY
INTELLIGENCE SUMMARY.
(Erase heading not required.)

Army Form C. 2118

Place	Date	Hour	Summary of Events and Information	Remarks and references to Appendices
CAISTRE	cont.d 11-8-15		Hondeghem and Hazebrouck. Enormous area, impossible to supervise with only motorcycle methods of getting about (Motor Lorry (slow and expensive to Country) or Horse (slow and distance limited)	
		2.30 p.m	Search for Water with D.A.D.M.S. eventually had to go to Meteren. Permission to draw water from Brewery, Arkeren.	
	H.Qy	Well (? over 1500 ft. deep) continual supply. Excellent water.		
CAISTRE	12-8-15	8-45	Reported A.D.M.S. Arranged to supervise sanitation of Billets ete and to different Districts to supervise sanitation daily in Lorry to different Districts to supervise sanitation of Billets ete and to advise and test water supplies. Distributed Parties round Division.	
		10.30	Inspected H.Qrs. Billets ete. Great improvement in condition	
	H.Qy	5-15 p.m	Reported A.D.M.S. carried out water tests, results satisfactory.	
		8- 0 am	Left in Lorry with party of 12 N.C.O's 4 men for instruction at Westoutre. Reported A.D.M.S. 28th Division 9-45 am. Handed over to Sanitary Officer, Lieut. Draycott, to work with him.	
CAISTRE	13-8-15	H.Qy	Carried out inspections with I.S.O. and distributed party over district	

Army Form C. 2118

WAR DIARY
or
INTELLIGENCE SUMMARY.
(Erase heading not required.)

Instructions regarding War Diaries and Intelligence Summaries are contained in F. S. Regs., Part II. and the Staff Manual respectively. Title pages will be prepared in manuscript.

Place	Date	Hour	Summary of Events and Information	Remarks and references to Appendices
WEST OUTRE	13-8-15		Report of epidemic of diarrhoea at dressing stations of 11th Royal Warwicks & 6th East Lancashire Regiment. Went down at once to investigate matters with Lt Draycott. About 100 cases, probable cause from milk at adjoining farm, latter in most insanitary condition. Milk probably contaminated and also watered down with contaminated water. Arranged steps to be taken with M.O. Royal Warwicks.	
WEST OUTRE	14-8-15		Reported to Inspected various camps, bivouacs, tents most shelters, huts etc. mostly in roomy condition owing to continual occupancy and difficulty of keeping aired and swept. General sanitary arrangements good. Pail system of latrines where possible. Excreta burnt in special incinerators. Also a few horsfall incinerators working, not as satisfactory as local made ones. Bathing arrangements excellent – three "Baths" working. Clean change of clothing for each man after bath. Supplied on Sanitary Section. Water in truth as available, from streams and special (wood bordered) wells. (cont'd overleaf)	

WAR DIARY
INTELLIGENCE SUMMARY
(Erase heading not required.)

Army Form C. 2118

Place	Date	Hour	Summary of Events and Information	Remarks and references to Appendices
WESTOUTRE	cont 14.6.15		II Dirty & lousy clothing (under) disinfected by creasol or steam on mensers & tops washed and laundered either at Baths laundry by civilian women or at Convent, Loore. Any damp or repairing also done on premises.	
WESTOUTRE	15.6.15	9.17		
		9.30	Reported to ADMS 28th Division with D. Daycott Visited Divisions of 11th Royal Warwicks & 8th E. Lancs. Diarrhoea almost cleared. Inspected Bathing arrangements at Loore, also Coups of the Leicesh. Regiments, 37th Division, here for instruction. Condition only fair.	
WESTOUTRE	16.6.15	9.20	Reported with D. Daycott to ADMS, 28th Div. Visited & inspected Baths and arrangements at Dranoutre. Excellent. Water pumped (steam pump) from dammed stream. Saw new Water supply (pump) into field stream. Stream to Lake, in Chatean grounds. Lake tapped by R.E. with large cast iron piping and carried to suitable spot for refilling water carts. On and off by valve cock. Special men on duty at cock to prevent waste. *(contd. overleaf)*	

WAR DIARY
INTELLIGENCE SUMMARY

Army Form C. 2118

Place	Date	Hour	Summary of Events and Information	Remarks and references to Appendices
WESTOUTRE	16-8-15 cont		Sanitary Section O.B.O. of filling station for water testing etc. & team all water properly chlorinated.	
	17-8-15	5.30pm	Returned to CAISTRE having greatly benefited by visit	
CAISTRE	17-8-15	9-20	Reported ADMS. Gave verbal report of visit to WESTOUTRE. Inspected Hqrs Billets. Improvements about. 3.0 pm Inspected with Section Corporal Hqrs Billets, Cyclist Coy & Divisional Train generally good.	
CAISTRE	18-8-15	9-15 am	Reported ADMS. By lorry to HONDEGHEM. Inspected 124th Brigade R.F.A. conditions very fair. Advised on proposed change of Billet for "A" Battery & on sanitary arrangements to be made. Inspected Div. Ammunition Column. Conditions good. R.M.O. & Battery Officers taking great interest in Sanitation than England.	
CAISTRE	19-8-15	9-0am	Reported ADMS. Received instructions for making special features memento for burning of faeces and making Pit in hand. Inspected Hqrs area. Chopmany Manure Mound to be carted away to be spread out on land.	

WAR DIARY
INTELLIGENCE SUMMARY

Army Form C. 2118

Place	Date	Hour	Summary of Events and Information	Remarks and references to Appendices
CAISTRE	20-8-15	9.0 am	Reported to ADMS. Inspected Billets etc. 115th Brigade with M.O. and advised for measures to be taken to keep all in good sanitation sanitary condition.	
CAISTRE	21-8-15	9.0 am	Reported to ADMS Inspected Billets etc. 126th Brigade RFA with M.O. Made recommendations. Conditions generally good. Inspected 123rd Brigade R.F.A. with M.O. Found two billets in occupation with troops sleeping either partly partitioned off from big guns, or directly over, on stretchers, no bearing. Conditions damp and very unhealthy. Saw Brigade Rodent and recommended evacuation of Billets for little ones. Every attention given. This was agreed to and carried out.	
		8.0 pm	my advice	
CAISTRE	22-8-15	9.0 am	Reported to ADMS. Inspected Agra mess & found things going and	
CAISTRE	23-8-15	9.0 am	Reported to ADMS. Received instructions re special incidentulus. Instructions carried out. Went to Hazebrouck. Inspected Billets partly built French Hospital, occupied by Warwick Reg. & E. Lancs Regt.	

(cont'd overleaf)

Army Form C. 2118

WAR DIARY
or
INTELLIGENCE SUMMARY.
(Erase heading not required.)

Instructions regarding War Diaries and Intelligence Summaries are contained in F. S. Regs., Part II. and the Staff Manual respectively. Title pages will be prepared in manuscript.

Place	Date	Hour	Summary of Events and Information	Remarks and references to Appendices
CAISTRE	23-8-15 (cont'd)		General arrangements good. Improvements in hand being supervised by a member of Sanitary Section. Noticed a lot of unprotected from flying about & gave instructions for covering up. Flies very noticeable. Found troops billeted in poorly ventilated and damp cellars & had them immediately removed to above ground accommodation. Inspected Billets etc of Bedfordshire Regt near Staplehoek with M.O. and found all in good order. Also inspected Billets of Loyal North Lancs Regt & found conditions fair. Advised that several improvements should be made.	
CAISTRE	24-8-15	9.0 am	Reported to ADMS. Received certain instructions re move to new area. Improved on waiting parties of Gurkhas to remind Regiments that Billets, Latrines etc rough be cleaned up before leaving. 10.30 Went with ADMS to Bailleul. Visited Sanitary Exhibition. Some good ideas, other "pretty" but impracticable. Inspected Hosp. Area. Incinerator progressing	

Army Form C. 2118

WAR DIARY
INTELLIGENCE SUMMARY.
(Erase heading not required.)

Instructions regarding War Diaries and Intelligence Summaries are contained in F. S. Regs., Part II. and the Staff Manual respectively. Title pages will be prepared in manuscript.

XII

Place	Date	Hour	Summary of Events and Information	Remarks and references to Appendices
CAISTRE	25/8/15	8.30	DADMS called as usual. Reported to ADMS and received final instructions re entraining etc.	
CAISTRE	26/8/15	7.50	Went on Lorry to Cassel. Found out route and ground for bivouac.	
		2.45pm	Marched to Cassel, arriving 6.0 pm. Bivouaced. Reported to R.T.O. Cassel and made arrangements re morning.	
DOULLENS	27/8/15		Reported to R.T.O. Cassel 5.35 am. and entrained. Tram left Cassel route via HAZEBROUCK Jne., LILLERS, ST POL, FREVENT, DOULLENS to MARINCOURT - PAS. Arrived 3.15 pm., then had to march back 8 miles to LA VOIE DES PRES, DOULLENS. Found Billet, not at all satisfactory. Unit to be mixed with another Regiment. Had tents pitched. D.A.D.M.S. called 7.0 pm and reported arrival 15 pm.	
		7.30 pm	Lorry arrived having come by road with Field Ambulance Workshop Unit.	
DOULLENS	28/8/15	9.0 am	Reported to ADMS. Section on Water testing etc to-morrow.	
		4.30 pm	Reported to ADNS. Received instructions to investigate outbreak of Scabies of Batt. Lincolnshire Regt.	

WAR DIARY

INTELLIGENCE SUMMARY.

Army Form C. 2118

Place	Date	Hour	Summary of Events and Information	Remarks and references to Appendices
DOULLENS	29.8.15	8.30am	Sent Sectn to 9th Batt Leicesters Hd qrs of clothing etc of 90 men. Advised all ranks to biveher Billets	
		9 p.m	lousy and probably infected with scabies.	
DOULLENS	30.8.15	9.0 a.m	Reported DADMS. Divisional Area	
			Distributed Section over Divisional Area to supervise Sanitation etc. of all Units	
		11.0. pm	good. Units paying much more attention to Sanitary measures. Reports of visiting	
DOULLENS	31.8.15	9.0 a.m	DADMS. Inspected Hyb. Billets etc and found conditions bad. Made recommendations for immediate action & put A.C.C.	
		9 p.m	to supervise.	

37th Div.n
Summarised but not extracted
12/7/98

37th Div.n Sam. Section
Vol II

Sept 15

S
Sept 15

Confidential.

War Diary

of

O/C Sanitary Section
37th Division

from Sept. 1st 1915 to Sept. 30th 1915

H.G.Moog Lieut RAMC(T.F)
O/C

Army Form C. 2118.

WAR DIARY
INTELLIGENCE SUMMARY.
(Erase heading not required.)

Instructions regarding War Diaries and Intelligence Summaries are contained in F. S. Regs. Part II. and the Staff Manual respectively. Title pages will be prepared in manuscript.

Place	Date	Hour	Summary of Events and Information	Remarks and references to Appendices
DOULLENS	1-9-15		Reported to ADMS. Received instructions re move to PAS. Went on Lorry to PAS and inspected prospective Billets &c.	
DOULLENS	2-9-15	2.0 pm	Reported to ADMS. Received instructions for two men to be sent to WARLINCOURT to supervise Sanitation, and re filling of Water Carts etc. at new Water Station. Received instructions re move to PAS.	
DOULLENS	3-9-15	9.0 am	Reported to ADMS. Lorry to Mondicourt. Saw Major Watson O/C 48th Field Amb. re Sanitation and Water Supply at Hospital & Billets, Pas. arranged to meet at PAS afternoon. Saw good Incinerator for disposal of rubbish manual execute &c & noted construction. Went to Water Station, WARLINCOURT. Made Inspection. Left 2 men in charge concerning arrangements and re filling. Water excellent, hill spring, abundantly clear, colourless, and free from contamination. Arrangements being made by R.E. Chief History. 2.45 pm Met Major Watson at PAS and advised on best methods of Sanitation to it adopted and advised on Billets.	

Army Form C. 2118.

WAR DIARY
INTELLIGENCE SUMMARY.
(Erase heading not required.)

Instructions regarding War Diaries and Intelligence Summaries are contained in F. S. Regs., Part II. and the Staff Manual respectively. Title pages will be prepared in manuscript.

Place	Date	Hour	Summary of Events and Information	Remarks and references to Appendices
DOULLENS	4-9-15	9.0 am	Reported to ADMS. result of visit to WARLINCOURT and PAS.	
		10.0 am	Accompanied ADMS on visit of inspection to FONQUEVILLERS. Village badly shelled. Living quarters compelled to be in cellars and shell proof dug-outs.	
DOULLENS	5-9-15	1.30 pm	Reported to ADMS. Accompanied him & DADMS to PAS. Inspected Billets for self and Section and made arrangements for to-morrow. Went to WARLINCOURT and inspected Water Station and found all satisfactory	
PAS.	6-9-15	9.0 am	Proceeded by road to PAS. 11-45 Reported arrival to DADMS	
		2.0 pm	Inspected Town and made arrangements re Sanitary measures to be put in hand.	
PAS	7-9-15	6.30 am	Full inspection of Town made by Section 9.15 Reported to DADMS and received instructions re clearing up of Town etc.	
		2.0 pm	Reported ADMS and arranged distribution of Section to contact Divisional Area. Received request from M.O. ¾ 126 Brigade RFA to advise on Latrine positions for his Brigade	

T2134. Wt. W708—776. 500000. 4/15. Sir J. C. & S.

Army Form C. 2118.

WAR DIARY
INTELLIGENCE SUMMARY.
(Erase heading not required.)

Instructions regarding War Diaries and Intelligence Summaries are contained in F. S. Regs., Part II. and the Staff Manual respectively. Title pages will be prepared in manuscript.

Place	Date	Hour	Summary of Events and Information	Remarks and references to Appendices
PAS	8-9-15	8.45	Reported to ADMS. Distributed Section, one Squad to HENU, one Squad to HUMBERCAMP, for duties in respective Districts. Took over an issue of all Disinfectants and also preparation & issue of Izyntree helmet solution. One man from each Battalion attached to Section for Divisional Sanitary Work.	
PAS	9-9-15	8.45	Reported to ADMS. Received instructions. Visited quarters occupied by 126 Brigade R.F.A. at HENU, ST AMAND, GAUDIENPRE, with M.O. 7c.	
		2.0	Reported to DADMS. Visited Batteries of 126 Brigade R.F.A. and also Billets occupied by Gunners. Conditions very satisfactory.	
PAS	10-9-15	8.45	ADMS Received instructions. Inspected district of HENU, spend sanitary measures in hand.	
PAS	11-9-15	8.45	Reported to DADMS for instructions. Inspected Billets etc. of 1st Fusiliers Transport and advised measures to be taken.	
		2.0	Reported to ADMS. Inspected district of POMMIER. Satisfactory	
PAS	12-9-15	11-0 am	Saw ADMS & DADMS re Disinfectants. 3.30 Visited by O.C. No. 9 Mobile Laboratory & went with him to ADMS re Water testing.	

Army Form C. 2118.

WAR DIARY
INTELLIGENCE SUMMARY.
(Erase heading not required.)

Instructions regarding War Diaries and Intelligence Summaries are contained in F. S. Regs., Part II. and the Staff Manual respectively. Title pages will be prepared in manuscript.

Place	Date	Hour	Summary of Events and Information	Remarks and references to Appendices
PAS.	13-9-15	9-0 am	Reported to ADMS for instructions. 10-0 am Visited BERLES to inspect Wells at request of M.O. 8th Leicesters. Arrived on Well in RAVIN behind trenches and took sample for analysis.	
PAS.	14-9-15	9-45	Reported to ADMS for instructions. Accompanied G/B Reg Mobile Laboratory to inspect wells at BIENVILLERS. Took samples from suitable wells and advised M.O's as to necessary sterilization and protection required. Visited Water Station, WARLINCOURT, Satisfactory. Improvements in hand.	
PAS.	15-9-15	8-45	AMS. Proceeded to BIENVILLERS inspected with MOs Billets and Sanitary areas occupied by 9th Batt. Leicester Regt. Very satisfactory. Discussed question of centralysed Sanitary areas and alloted positions for use of 7th & 9th Batt. Leicester Regt at BIENVILLERS. 3-0 Visited MO/c 6th Batt. Leicester Regt BERLES and advised C.O. re use of wells in village.	
PAS	16-9-15	9-0	ADMS. 3-0 Accompanied ADMS to BERLES & in conjunction with MO/c inspected area occupied by 6th Leicester Regt. Gave instructions for clearing up to be done forthwith.	

Army Form C. 2118.

WAR DIARY
INTELLIGENCE SUMMARY.
(Erase heading not required.)

Place	Date	Hour	Summary of Events and Information	Remarks and references to Appendices
PAS	17-9-15	9.0 A.D.M.S.	Discussed question of centralized Sanitary area	
PAS	18-9-15	8.45 A.D.M.S.	9.30 Proceeded to BERLES + with M.O. 6th Lancasters inspected Trenches. Also advised on Water Supply at Dugouts in Ravine. Arranged for all Billets to be thoroughly clean and disinfected while troops in trenches. Inspected Billets at HUMBERCAMP and reported the unhealthy condition thereof to M.O. 13th Fusiliers	
PAS	19-9-15	8.45 A.D.M.S.	Inspected + advised on Wells at MONDICOURT	
PAS	20-9-15	9.0 A.D.M.S.	Proceeded to HANNESCAMPS. Inspected, advised, and reported on condition of wells. Sanitary conditions satisfactory Proceeded to HUMBERCAMP + with M.O. 13th Fusiliers, inspected wells Billets etc occupied by his Unit. Satisfactory	
PAS	21-9-15	9.0 A.D.M.S.	Proceeded to GRENAS + with M.O. Div Ammunition Column inspected Billets, Horse lines etc., and made recommendations.	
		2.45 p.m.	St AMAND made general inspection. Work going on slowly	
		5.30	Took samples of water from Horse Troughs and pickled Lead in morning. Trace found, from pulley through put out of action	

Army Form C. 2118.

WAR DIARY
or
INTELLIGENCE SUMMARY.
(Erase heading not required.)

Instructions regarding War Diaries and Intelligence Summaries are contained in F.S. Regs., Part II. and the Staff Manual respectively. Title pages will be prepared in manuscript.

Place	Date	Hour	Summary of Events and Information	Remarks and references to Appendices
PAS	22-9-15	8.45 ADMS	10-0 am to FAMECHON. Made investigation into outbreak of Enteric Fever amongst Civilian population. Advised precautions to be taken and ordered necessary disinfection.	
		2.30 pm	MONDICOURT. Inspected with MO % all Billets etc. used by troops in neighbourhood. Made recommendations.	
PAS	23-9-15	9-0 am ADMS	10-0 am Proceeded to FONCQUEVILLERS. Inspected Sanitation of areas occupied by 37th Division. 11.30 Proceeded to Div. Water Station, WARLINCOURT, and found general arrangements greatly improved.	
PAS	24-9-15	8.45 ADMS	Made preparations to move at short notice.	
PAS.	25-9-15	9-0 ADMS	Awaiting orders.	
PAS	26-9-15	9-0 ADMS	2-0 Proceeded to LA CAUCHIE, and with MO % 123 Brigade RFA inspected and advised on wells.	
PAS	27-9-15	9-0 ADMS	Inspected Billets in PAS area.	
PAS	28-9-15	9-0 ADMS	Proceeded to BEAUVAL & saw No 9 Mobile Laboratory.	
PAS	29-9-15	9-0 ADMS	Visited HENU, ST AMAND, POMMIER, HUMBERCAMP. Too wet to inspect much.	
PAS	30-9-15	9-0 ADMS	Made further inspection at PAS. Visited HUMBERCAMP in afternoon.	

Summarised but not copied
12/7595

37th Div: San: Sectn.
Vol: 3

Oct 15

Oct 1915

Confidential.

War Diary

of

Sanitary Section, 37th Division, B.E.F.

From Oct 1: 1915 to Oct. 31: 1915

H. Gihnos
Lieut.
O/Commanding

Army Form C. 2118.

WAR DIARY
INTELLIGENCE SUMMARY.
(Erase heading not required.)

Instructions regarding War Diaries and Intelligence Summaries are contained in F. S. Regs., Part II. and the Staff Manual respectively. Title pages will be prepared in manuscript.

Place	Date	Hour	Summary of Events and Information	Remarks and references to Appendices
PAS	1-10-15	9-0	A.D.M.S. Inspected Billets etc in PAS. 2.0 Inspected Billets etc. GAUDIEMPRE.	
PAS	2-10-15	9-0	A.D.M.S. Made inspection of Water Status. WARLINCOURT. Satisfactory. 2-0 Inspected district of St AMAND, unsatisfactory. Took steps to get matters improved.	
PAS	3-10-15	9-0	A.D.M.S. Proceeded to HUMBERCAMP & saw N.C.O. i/c Squad re areas for Central Latrines. 2-0 HUMBERCAMP inspected Billets etc. occupied by 11 ROY. WARWICK REGT. satisfactory.	
PAS	4-10-15	9-0	A.D.M.S. 10-0 Proceeded to BIENVILLERS & HANNESCAMPS and inspected and advised on Wells.	
PAS	5-10-15	9-0	A.D.M.S. 10-0 Proceeded to HUMBERCAMP. Inspected with M.O. i/c Billets etc occupied by 6 BEDS. REGT. satisfactory. Investigated village water tanks at buildings used as Divisional Baths, and advised closing up of same.	
PAS	6-10-15	9-0	A.D.M.S. 10-0 Proceeded to LA BAZEQUE and inspected with M.O. i/c area occupied by 124 Brigade R.F.A. Condition fair. Made recommendation. HUMBERCAMP. Went over areas selected for Central Latrines.	

Army Form C. 2118.

WAR DIARY
INTELLIGENCE SUMMARY
(Erase heading not required.)

Instructions regarding War Diaries and Intelligence Summaries are contained in F.S. Regs., Part II. and the Staff Manual respectively. Title pages will be prepared in manuscript.

Place	Date	Hour	Summary of Events and Information	Remarks and references to Appendices
PAS	7-10-15	9-0 ADMS	Proceeded to ACHEUX. Saw Sanitary Officer, 4th DIVISION and compared notes.	
PAS	8-10-15	9-0 ADMS	Proceeded to HUMBERCAMP and saw senior M.O. re latrines near	
PAS	9-10-15	9-0 ADMS	Proceeded to HENU. Inspected Billets etc occupied by 126 Brigade RFA, 125 Brigade RFA. General condition good.	
PAS	10-10-15	9-0 ADMS	Proceeded to SOUASTRE. Inspected Billets etc occupied by 19th Batt R.G.A. Unsatisfactory. Made recommendations & sent report to DDMS. Made tour of area just taken up by 10 Fusiliers. Rooms satisfactory	
PAS	11-10-15	9-0 ADMS	Proceeded to WARLINCOURT and with MO/c inspected Billets occupied by DIVISIONAL TRAIN. Generally satisfactory	
PAS	12-10-15	9-15 ADMS	Proceeded to BIENVILLERS and with MO/c inspected & used occupied by 10 BEDS. REGT. Satisfactory. Rooms good	
PAS	13-10-15	9-0 ADMS	Proceeded to AMIENS to draw stores.	
PAS	14-10-15	10-30 ADMS	Proceeded to BERLES. Inspected & advised re Well in trenches over occupied by 13 RIFLE BRIGADE. Made several	
		2-0	Inspected with MO/c recommendations.	

Army Form C. 2118.

WAR DIARY
or
INTELLIGENCE SUMMARY.
(Erase heading not required.)

Instructions regarding War Diaries and Intelligence Summaries are contained in F.S. Regs., Part II. and the Staff Manual respectively. Title pages will be prepared in manuscript.

Place	Date	Hour	Summary of Events and Information	Remarks and references to Appendices
PAS	15-10-15	9-0 ADMS	Orderly Room and clerical work.	
PAS.	16-10-15	9-0 ADMS		
		10-0	Proceeded to WARLINCOURT and investigated cases of Ice and made recommendations. Inspected Water Station. satisfactory	
		2.15	Proceeded to GAUDIEMPRE and inspected area occupied by Supply Section, Divisional Train, and ENTRENCHING BATT. Progress satisfactory	
PAS	17-10-15	9-0 ADMS	Instructions re Vidange. Clerical work.	
PAS	18-10-15	9-0 DADMS	9.30 Interviewed Mayor & Chef des Contonniers re cleansing of Town & removal of refuse. Authorities unable to carry on work. Arrangement made to work with military assistance regularly.	
		9-0 DADMS	Orderly Room. 1.15 Proceeded to SEAMAND and with M.O. 7/c inspected areas occupied by 13 RIFLE BRIGADE. Fairly satisfactory	
PAS	19-10-15		Made recommendations.	
PAS	20-10-15	9-0 ADMS		
		10-0	Proceeded to La CAUCHÉ. Inspected area occupied by 123 Brigade R.F.A. Generally satisfactory. Made report on few unsatisfactory conditions requiring attention	
		2-0	Proceeded to BIENVILLERS and inspected area occupied by (cont'd over)	

WAR DIARY
INTELLIGENCE SUMMARY.
(Erase heading not required.)

Place	Date	Hour	Summary of Events and Information	Remarks and references to Appendices
PAS	20.10.15 (contd)		4th LEICESTER REGT. Condition good. Made recommendations.	
PAS	21.10.15	9.0 ADMS 9.45	Proceeded to TAMECHON and with MO/c inspected area occupied by YORKSHIRE DRAGOONS. Conditions good.	
		2.0	Proceeded to SOUASTRE and inspected area occupied by 153 Field Co RE., conditions bad, saw OC and recommended alterations required, Ordnance Workshops — progress satisfactory, 147 Army Troops RE, progress satisfactory, 125 Brigade R.F.A. — satisfactory, saw M.O. of Battery, also 4 other Units, and recommended work to be done	
PAS	22.10.15	9.0 ADMS 9.30	Proceeded to TAMECHON, saw O/C YORKSHIRE DRAGOONS re closing up of Urinal near Cookhouse. Proceeded to MONDICOURT + with MO/c inspected areas occupied by DIVISIONAL SUPPLY COLUMN, MOBILE VETERINARY SECTION, MOTOR MACHINE GUN SECTION, and details RE. General conditions good. Made recommendations.	
		2.0	Proceeded to BERLES, found 8 LEICESTER REGT taking up quarters #G/y necessary sanitary measures will in hand	

WAR DIARY
INTELLIGENCE SUMMARY
(Erase heading not required.)

Army Form C. 2118.

Instructions regarding War Diaries and Intelligence Summaries are contained in F. S. Regs., Part II. and the Staff Manual respectively. Title pages will be prepared in manuscript.

Place	Date	Hour	Summary of Events and Information	Remarks and references to Appendices
PAS	23-10-15	9-0	ADMS 10-0 Proceeded to GRENAS and with MO%, inspected area occupied by DIVISIONAL AMMUNITION COLUMN. Generally satisfactory. Reported on alterations required.	
		2-0	Proceeded to HUMBERCAMP and with MO%, inspected area of 9 LEICESTER REGT. Conditions unsatisfactory owing to shortage of timber etc. R.E. latrine seats attention trenches etc not for sanitary work. Reported matter to ADMS for attention. 4 Only feet available.	
PAS	24-10-15	9-15	ADMS 10-0 to SOUASTRE. Saw MO%, 6 EAST LANCS REGT and inspected area. Pointed out many alterations requiring immediate attention. Reported to ADMS re Manure heaps (removal of), re removal of old straw in Billets, re lack of suitable storage for food. Interview with C.R.E. re supply of timber for sanitary work.	
			Result unsatisfactory	
PAS	25-10-15	9-0	ADMS 10-0 Inspected Road Conflict dug out and advised thereon. SOUASTRE Saw Transport Officer, 10 FUSILIERS and advised on Billets and sanitary work required to be done. (cont'd over)	

Army Form C. 2118.

WAR DIARY
INTELLIGENCE SUMMARY.
(Erase heading not required.)

Instructions regarding War Diaries and Intelligence Summaries are contained in F. S. Regs., Part II. and the Staff Manual respectively. Title pages will be prepared in manuscript.

Place	Date	Hour	Summary of Events and Information	Remarks and references to Appendices
PAS	25-10-15 (cont'd)		HUMBERCAMP. Saw MO i/c 10 LOYAL NORTH LANCS REGT and inspected area. Satisfactory. 2-0 ADMS Discussed matter of manure removal etc., also re increase Hy of fatigue party for sanitary work in Division. Very necessary.	
PAS	26-10-15	9-0 ADMS	Inspected PAS area. Satisfactory. 2-15 ST AMAND met MO i/c 11 ROYAL WARWICK REGT and inspected Area. Great #9hy lack of materials for satisfactory sanitary work.	
PAS	27-10-15	#9hy 9-0 ADMS	Instructions re Horsfall Destructor. Advised thereon.	
PAS	28-10-15	9-0 ADMS	Supervised assembling of Destructor. 10-15 MONDICOURT STATION Saw MB i/c 110 Co. RE re supervision inspected Railhead.	
PAS	29-10-15	9-0 ADMS	10-0 POMMIER Met MO i/c 124 Brigade RFA and advised re work required at Brigade Hq. BIENVILLERS. Inspected new latrine shelters #9hy Inspected Water Station. WARLINCOURT. Gave orders re Sanitary arrangements. Met MO i/c Destruct.	
PAS	30-10-15	9-0 ADMS	10-0 GAUDIEMPRE Selected site for Destructor Supply Section ASC. and inspected area. Satisfactory except Supply section Made investigations into east of Latrine Farm and advised disposal of #9hy to Latrine.	
PAS	31-10-15	#9hy 9-0 ADMS	Saw DIVISIONAL TRAIN re Sanitary squad for Supply Section.	

T2134. Wt. W708—776. 500000. 4/15. Sir J. C. & S.

37th Bri. San: Sect.
Vol 4

Summarised but not copied

121/7635

Nov 15

S
Nov 1915

Confidential.

War Diary

of

Sanitary Section,
37th Division B.E.F.

from Nov. 1st 1915 to Nov. 30th 1915

H.S. Gross
Lieut

Army Form C. 2118

WAR DIARY
INTELLIGENCE SUMMARY.
(Erase heading not required.)

Instructions regarding War Diaries and Intelligence Summaries are contained in F. S. Regs., Part II. and the Staff Manual respectively. Title pages will be prepared in manuscript.

Place	Date	Hour	Summary of Events and Information	Remarks and references to Appendices
PAS	1-11-15	9-0 ADMS	Instructions re Well at BIENVILLERS. 10-0 Proceeded to B, inspected well, supply of water small. Called at GAUDIEMPRE, gave instructions re building of Horsfall Destructor.	
PAS	2-11-15	9-0 ADMS	10-0 Accompanied O/C MOBILE LAB. to BIENVILLERS and made further inspection of Well.	
PAS	3-11-15	9-0 ADMS	Proceeded to ST AMAND and made general inspection. Proceeded to BERLES and with MO/c made inspection of Billets etc occupied by 6th LEICESTER REGT. Drying shed being built.	
PAS	4-11-15	9-0 ADMS	10-0 Proceeded to SOUASTRE and with MO/c inspected Billets, Transport lines etc. of 10th R.FUSILIERS. Proceeded to ST AMAND, saw MO/c 126 Bde R.F.A. re supervision of various Transport lines in village. 2-0 Proceeded to ST AMAND & with M.O./c 126 Bde R.F.A. inspected Horse Lines of 10 L.N. LANCS. REGT, & E LANCS REGT, 11 R WARWICK REGT, 13 R FUSILIERS REGT, 13 RIFLE BDE, 6 BEDS. REGT. and gave instructions for necessary sanitary work to be done.	
PAS	5-11-15	9-0 ADMS.	Visited WATER STATION. 2.30 Proceeded to HUMBERCAMP and with MO/c inspected Billets occupied by 13 RIFLE BRIGADE.	

T2134. Wt. W708—776. 500000. 4/15. Sir J. C. & S.

Army Form C. 2118

WAR DIARY
or
INTELLIGENCE SUMMARY.
(Erase heading not required.)

Instructions regarding War Diaries and Intelligence Summaries are contained in F. S. Regs., Part II. and the Staff Manual respectively. Title pages will be prepared in manuscript.

Place	Date	Hour	Summary of Events and Information	Remarks and references to Appendices
PAS	6-11-15	9.0	A.D.M.S. 10-0 Proceeded to GAUDIEMPRE and with M.O%c # ENTRENCHING BATT. made general inspection of village. Investigated case of enteric fever (civilian) and made recommendations.	
PAS	7-11-15	9.0	A.D.M.S. 10-0 Proceeded to BUS saw Sanitary Officer, 46th DIVISION, and gained useful information.	
PAS	8-11-15	9.0	A.D.M.S. 2-0 Proceeded to POMMIER and with M.O%c inspected all Units in village & advised on sanitary measures required to be taken.	
PAS	9-11-15	9.0	A.D.M.S. Received instructions re Sanitary work required for Divisional Prison, HERTEBISE FARM. 9.30 Proceeded to FARM and advised on sanitary work required.	
PAS	10-11-15	9.0	A.D.M.S. 9-45 Proceeded to HENU & made inspection of all wells. 1-45 Proceeded to ST AMAND & made inspection of all wells.	
PAS	11-11-15	9.0	A.D.M.S. 10-0 Proceeded to BIENVILLERS and with M.O%c inspected Billets etc of 6th BEDS. REGT. Very satisfactory. All Billets being cleared of old straw. 2-0 With M.O%c inspected Billets etc of 9th LEICESTER REGT	

Army Form C. 2118.

WAR DIARY
INTELLIGENCE SUMMARY.
(Erase heading not required.)

Instructions regarding War Diaries and Intelligence Summaries are contained in F. S. Regs., Part II. and the Staff Manual respectively. Title pages will be prepared in manuscript.

Place	Date	Hour	Summary of Events and Information	Remarks and references to Appendices
PAS	12-11-15	9-0 AoSms	Proceeded to SOUASTRE and obtained new Billets for AyrLs Squad to be moved from HENU to SOUASTRE. Latter for central for area. 3-0 Visited DIV. WATER STATION. Went on approaches/roadways	
PAS	13-11-15	9-0 ASms	10-0 Proceeded to POMMIER and obtained new Billet for Squad from HUMBERCAMPS. Arranged for latrining. Inspected all wells at POMMIER and made records.	
PAS	14-11-15	9-0 HoSms	Inspected Sanitary arrangements at DIV. DETENTION BARRACKS, HERTEBISE FARM. Satisfactory.	
PAS	15-11-15	9-0 ASms	10-0 Proceeded to HUMBERCAMPS. Area in satisfactory condition. 1-45 to LA CAUCHIE. Made inspection record of all wells.	
PAS	16-11-15	9-30 ASms	10-0 Proceeded to LA HERLIERE and made inspection record of all wells.	
PAS	17-11-15	9-30 ASms	10-0 to LA CAUCHIE and with MO/o made inspection of gun lines of 123 Brigade R.F.A. Conditions satisfactory. Sanitation good.	
PAS	18-11-15	9-30 ASms	10.30 to MONDICOURT. Inspected Billets etc of 10 LABOUR BATTN. Recommended work to be done to make billets more healthy	

Army Form C. 2118

WAR DIARY
INTELLIGENCE SUMMARY.
(Erase heading not required.)

Instructions regarding War Diaries and Intelligence Summaries are contained in F.S. Regs., Part II. and the Staff Manual respectively. Title pages will be prepared in manuscript.

Place	Date	Hour	Summary of Events and Information	Remarks and references to Appendices
PAS	19-11-15	9.30 aDms. 10.0 to HANNESCAMPS. General inspection. Investigated Wells. 2.30 made inspection of areas occupied by Hqs. Units.	
PAS	20-11-15	9.30 ADms 10.0 to HANNESCAMPS. With MO/c made inspection of Dug Outs etc occupied by 13 FUSILIERS. Under circumstances, conditions satisfactory	
PAS	21-11-15	9.30 ADms 11.0 to MONDICOURT & HURTEBISE FARM. Satisfactory. 3-0 to MONDICOURT saw G/C 10 LABOUR BATTN re improvements required to Billets.	
PAS	22-11-15	9.30 ADms 10-0 to BERLES. Inspected Billets etc of 8 LEICESTER REGT. Made recommendations for vacation of overcrowded & unhealthy Billets.	
PAS	23-11-15	9.30 ADms. 9-45 to SODASTRE. Inspected KINGS ROYAL RIFLES Transport lines & Billets. Generally satisfactory. Advised removal of troops from two unsatisfactory Billets.	
PAS	24-11-15	9.30 ADms. 10-45 to SODASTRE. Inspected with MO/c, Billets etc of 8 EAST LANCS REGT. Satisfactory. Inspected with MO/c Batteries of 125 Brigade RFA. Some Dug Outs (cont'd over)	

T2134. Wt. W708—776. 500000. 4/15. Sir J. C. & S.

Army Form C. 2118

WAR DIARY
or
INTELLIGENCE SUMMARY.
(Erase heading not required.)

Instructions regarding War Diaries and Intelligence Summaries are contained in F. S. Regs., Part II. and the Staff Manual respectively. Title pages will be prepared in manuscript.

Place	Date	Hour	Summary of Events and Information	Remarks and references to Appendices
PAS	24-11-15	contd	in very unhealthy conditions owing to wet & frost. Recommended immediate removal pending reconstruction. Sanitary arra good	
		2.30	With MO I/c area inspected all small Units at SOUASTRE. The Advised on alterations required to make Billets more healthy.	
PAS	25-11-15	4 Coy	General conditions good	
		9.0 ADMS	Visited GAUDIEMPRE and advised on alterations required	
			to HORSTALL DESTRUCTOR. This destructor consumes all refuse of troops	
			in village. Visited Water Station & gave instructions re precaution	
		4 Coy	to take with pipe-line owing to frost.	
PAS	26-11-15	9.0 ADMS 9.45	to SOUASTRE Saw NCO I/c Sqard re orders to battalion	
			to in village. Proceeded to ST AMAND Advised on Sanitary arrange-	
			ments required at Div. Theatre.	
		4 Coy 2.0	to POMMIER General inspection. Work proceeding satisfactorily	
PAS	27-11-15	9.30 ADMS 10.30	With MO I/c made inspection of Billets etc of	
		4 Coy	12th Brigade RFA gun-lines. Very satisfactory	

Army Form C. 2118

WAR DIARY
INTELLIGENCE SUMMARY.
(Erase heading not required.)

Instructions regarding War Diaries and Intelligence Summaries are contained in F. S. Regs., Part II. and the Staff Manual respectively. Title pages will be prepared in manuscript.

Place	Date	Hour	Summary of Events and Information	Remarks and references to Appendices
PAS	28-11-15	9.30 ADMS	Investigated cess pool under Barn occupied as Billet.	
		2.30	To GAUDIEMPRE re disinfection of dwelling after case of scarlet fever	
PAS	29-11-15	9.30 ADMS 10-0	Visited FONCQUEVILLERS and with MO ⅔ inspected Billets, Dug outs etc of B E LANCS REGT. General conditions good. Dug outs require better ventilation. Recommendation made.	
PAS.	30-11-15	9.30 DADMS	Visited Div. WATER STATION and gave instructions re disinfection of stove ends & Barrels	

S — Summarised but not copied

27th Answer

27th Jan: Dec:
vol: 5

F/2611.

13/
1928

December 1915

Confidential.

War Diary
of
Sanitary Section, 37th Division

from Dec 1st 1915 to Dec 31st 1915

(Volume V)

Army Form C. 2118

WAR DIARY
of
INTELLIGENCE SUMMARY.
(Erase heading not required.)

Instructions regarding War Diaries and Intelligence Summaries are contained in F. S. Regs., Part II. and the Staff Manual respectively. Title pages will be prepared in manuscript.

Place	Date	Hour	Summary of Events and Information	Remarks and references to Appendices
PAS	1-12-15	9.30	DADMS Proceeded to LABAZEQUE and LA BAZEQUE FARM & with MO Y/c inspected Billets etc occupied by 124 Brigade R.F.A. Very satisfactory. Excellent bathing huts erected by these Units.	
		2.30	with DADMS visited LAHERLIERE, saw O/C, Adjutant & MO Y/c 20th LIVERPOOL REGT. Advised on necessary sanitary measures to be taken	
PAS	2-12-15	9.30	DADMS Proceeded to LA BAZEQUE and accompanied MO Y/c 124 Brigade R.F.A. on tour of inspection of A, D & C Batteries. "A" & "D" in Dug outs satisfactory. "C" in Billets. Reported on repairs required to latter to render habitable.	
		9.30	DADMS Proceeded to BIENVILLERS & with MO Y/c inspected Billet & Dug-outs occupied by "B" Batt. 124 Brigade R.F.A. Billets very good. Dug outs very wet, to be evacuated.	
PAS	3-12-15	10.0		
PAS	4-12-15	9.30	DADmS Proceeded to POMMIER & with MO Y/c inspected Wagon Lines of 110th Brigade & 24th MANCHESTER REGT. Men in canvas Huts & Billets satisfactory. Had cases of overcrowded Billets put in order	
		2.30	Inspected & advised on Billets in PAS.	

WAR DIARY
INTELLIGENCE SUMMARY.
(Erase heading not required.)

Army Form C. 2118.

Place	Date	Hour	Summary of Events and Information	Remarks and references to Appendices
PAS	5-12-15	9.30 DADMS	10-15 to BERLES. Inspected Billets just vacated by 24th Manchester Regt. Left in very dirty condition. Surrounding trenches fouled. Reported thereon, also to effect that Billets are unfit for use unless put in better condition.	
		H.Qrs 2-0	Visited Water Station. Satisfactory	
PAS.	6-12-15	9.30 DADMS	10-0 to ST AMAND General inspection of sanitary areas	
		H.Qrs	Saw Capt Evans 48th F. AMBULANCE re case of infectious disease.	
PAS	7-12-15	9.30 DADMS	10-0 to ST ANAND approved position for Latrine shelters. Saw Guth House arranged by KINGS ROYAL RIFLE REGT. Excellent	
			2.30 Inspected Road Control dug outs HENU & GAUDIEMPRE. Very unsatisfactory. Men to be at once moved into Billets.	
PAS	8-12-15	9.30 ADMS	10-0 to ST AMAND Advised on several questions of sanitation. Proceeded to BERLES Inspected Billets etc recently occupied by 24th MANCHESTER REGT. Now satisfactorily cleaned up.	
		H.Qrs 2.30	Visited Water Station.	

Army Form C. 2118.

WAR DIARY
INTELLIGENCE SUMMARY.
(Erase heading not required.)

SANITARY SECTION,
XXXVII Division
1st LONDON (CITY OF LONDON) SANITARY Co.

Instructions regarding War Diaries and Intelligence Summaries are contained in F. S. Regs., Part II. and the Staff Manual respectively. Title pages will be prepared in manuscript.

Place	Date	Hour	Summary of Events and Information	Remarks and references to Appendices
PAS	9-12-15	9.30	A.D.M.S. 10.0 Inspected sanitary arrangements at PAS	
		1.45	Proceeded to BIENVILLERS & made further inspection of bad Billet occupied by 12 Brigade R.F.A. "D" Battery. Reported thereon	
PAS	10-12-15	9.30	A.D.M.S. 10.0 to LAHERLIERE. Inspected Billets etc. occupied by 20th LIVERPOOL REGT. Made recommendations to C.O. & M.O./c.	
PAS	11-12-15	9.30	A.D.M.S. 10.30 to HENU. Made inspection of Billets etc in village	
		3.0	to GAUDIEMPRE. Saw O/C AMMUNITION COLUMN, 16th BRIGADE R.G.A. re provision of new Water Cart	
PAS	12-12-15	9.45	A.D.M.S. received instructions re well at PAS and made investigation	
		2.45	to SOUASTRE. Called on O/c 3rd LABOUR BATTN re bad Billets of Section at HENU.	
PAS	13-12-15	9.30	A.D.M.S. 10.0 to BIENVILLERS re changing of positions of latrine shelters. Inspected sanitary areas of 9th LEICESTER REGT.	
PAS	14-12-15	9.30	A.D.M.S. 10.0 SOUASTRE. Saw 154 Co RE re latrine shelters for HUMBERCAMPS.	

Army Form C. 2118

SANITARY SECTION,
XXVII Division
1ST LONDON (CITY OF LONDON) SANITARY CO.

WAR DIARY
INTELLIGENCE SUMMARY.
(Erase heading not required.)

Instructions regarding War Diaries and Intelligence Summaries are contained in F. S. Regs., Part II. and the Staff Manual respectively. Title pages will be prepared in manuscript.

Place	Date	Hour	Summary of Events and Information	Remarks and references to Appendices
PAS	15-12-15	9-30 ADMS with MO i/c	10-15 to GAUDIEMPRE Inspected all Billets etc in village Generally satisfactory.	
PAS	16-12-15	9-30 ADMS with MO i/c	10-0 to La CAUCHIE Inspected all Billets etc in village & reported on unsatisfactory ones.	
PAS	17-12-15	9-30 ADMS with MO i/c	10-0 to HUMBERCAMPS & with MO i/c inspected Billets etc of 10th LOYAL NORTH LANCS. Condition good. Reported on a few unhealthy Barns	
PAS	18-12-15	9-30 ADMS with MO i/c	10-0 to MONDICOURT & with MO i/c inspected all Billets etc in village. Very satisfactory.	
PAS	19-12-15	9-30 ADMS with MO i/c	Visited Water Station & reported on work required to pumps & pipe line.	
PAS	20-12-15	9-30 ADMS with MO i/c	10-0 Visited Water Station. Inspected Road Conduit Pool. Dug out condemned & dirt supplied. Visited HUMBERCAMPS called on MO i/c 6th BEDFORDSHIRE REGT re structural condition of Billets & re provision of new Latrine Shelter	

T2134. Wt. W708—776. 500000. 4/15. Sir J. C. & S.

Army Form C. 2118.

SANITARY SECTION
XXVII Division
1ST LONDON (CITY OF LONDON) SANITARY C

WAR DIARY
INTELLIGENCE SUMMARY
(Erase heading not required.)

Instructions regarding War Diaries and Intelligence Summaries are contained in F. S. Regs., Part II. and the Staff Manual respectively. Title pages will be prepared in manuscript.

Place	Date	Hour	Summary of Events and Information	Remarks and references to Appendices
PAS	21-12-15	9.30 ADMS	10-0 to WARLINCOURT. Inspected with M.O.Y.C Billets etc occupied by DIVISIONAL TRAIN. Satisfactory. Proceeded to GRINCOURT & with M.O.Y.C inspected Billets etc of "D" Co. 9th NORTH STAFFS. REGT. Satisfactory. Improvised beds almost throughout.	HQ
PAS	22-12-15	9.30 ADMS	9-45 to HANNES CAMPS. With M.O.Y.C inspected Sanitary area. Unit just evacuated had left area in insanitary condition. Made report thereon.	HQ
PAS	23-12-15	9.30 ADMS	10-0 to BIENVILLERS. With M.O.Y.C inspected area occupied by 6th BEDS REGT. Satisfactory. Reported on some Billets in urgent need of repairs.	HQ
		2.30	Visited DIV. WATER STATION. Pumps faulty. Reported to R.E.	
PAS	24-12-15	9.30 ADMS	9-45 to HALLOY. Advised O/C "C" Co 10th LABOUR BATN on measures to take against lice.	HQ
PAS	25-12-15	9.30 ADMS		
PAS	26-12-15	9.30 ADMS	2-0 Visited Squads at SOUASTRE and POMMIER and settled questions of sanitation arising	HQ

WAR DIARY
INTELLIGENCE SUMMARY.
(Erase heading not required.)

Army Form C. 2118

Place	Date	Hour	Summary of Events and Information	Remarks and references to Appendices
PAS	27-12-15	9.30 A.M.	10-15 to BERLES. Inspected area just vacated by 20th LIVERPOOL REGT. Remainder of clearing up being done by Battalion in occupation. Inspected new R.E. Latrines, now in use.	
		2.30	to SOUASTRE. Saw R.E. re section of Latrines in areas	
PAS	28-12-15	9.30 A.M.	10-0 to SOUASTRE. With M.O.'s inspected Billets etc of 3rd LABOUR BATTN & 147 Coy. R.E. Satisfactory. Some billets requiring light letting into them. Shutter windows to be arranged for.	
		12-0	St AMAND. Inspected area occupied by 13th RIFLE BRIGADE Transport surroundings dirty. Gave orders for necessary work.	
PAS	29-12-15	9.30 A.M.	10-15 to ST AMAND Inspected Billets etc occupied by 55th HEAVY BATTERY, R.G.A. Satisfactory. With M.O.'s inspected Billets etc of 13th BATTN KINGS ROYAL RIFLES. General conditions good.	
PAS	30-12-15	9.30 A.M.	10-0 to HUMBERCAMPS With M.O.'s inspected Billets etc of 13th BATTN RIFLE BRIGADE. Reported on some requiring repairs General conditions satisfactory	

Army Form C. 2118.

SANITARY SECTION.
XXVII Division
1ST LONDON (CITY OF LONDON) SANITARY Co.

WAR DIARY
or
INTELLIGENCE SUMMARY.
(Erase heading not required.)

Instructions regarding War Diaries and Intelligence Summaries are contained in F. S. Regs., Part II. and the Staff Manual respectively. Title pages will be prepared in manuscript.

Place	Date	Hour	Summary of Events and Information	Remarks and references to Appendices
PAS	31-12-15		9-30 ADMS. 10-0 to Humbercamps. Advised on work required to Destructor. Inspected area occupied by M.T. Ammunition Column, 1st Battery, R.G.B.A. satisfactory. 2-15 to Famechon. Inspected Billets etc. of YORKSHIRE DRAGOONS and Hdqy 6th LIVERPOOL REGT. Very satisfactory	

37th Bri: L: San: Sec:
vol: 6

34th Sanys Schön

Jan. 1916

Confidential.

War Diary

of

Sanitary Section, 37th Division, B.E.F.

from Jan. 1st 1916 to Jan 31st 1916

(Volume VI)

E. Moss Capt
RAMC
O/C

Army Form C. 2118.

WAR DIARY
INTELLIGENCE SUMMARY.
(Erase heading not required.)

SANITARY SECTION,
XXXVIII Division
1ST LONDON (CITY OF LONDON) SANITARY Cº

Instructions regarding War Diaries and Intelligence Summaries are contained in F. S. Regs., Part II. and the Staff Manual respectively. Title pages will be prepared in manuscript.

Place	Date	Hour	Summary of Events and Information	Remarks and references to Appendices
PAS	1-1-16	9.30 A.M. 10.30	Insp^d Wagon Lines 125 Brigade RFA "B", "C" & "D" Batteries. "C" Battery in Barn next to Rly sdg with large hole in wall. Ordered latter to be repaired at once. Arranged for H^{rs}Gly Pail Latrines, ground at disposal being limited	H.G.hy
PAS	2-1-16	9.30 A.M.	Went through Reports etc	H.G.hy
PAS	3-1-16	9.30 A.M. 9.45 3.30	9.45 to BIENVILLERS. Took sample from well in clos/adjoining to large latrine. With M.O/c inspected Billets etc of 13th KINGS ROYAL RIFLES. Satisfactory. Informed M.O/c 9th LEICESTER REGT. re disinfection for case of Scarlet Fever & made arrangements to carry out necessary work. Inspected new Billets just taken up at PAS and advised on sanitary measures to be taken.	H.G.hy
PAS	4-1-16	9.30 A.M. 10-0 2.30	10-0 to GRENAS. With MO/c inspected all Billets etc occupied by 37th Divn AMMUNITION COLUMN. A few items requiring repairs. Reported same. Conditions vy good. Visited Water Station. Inspected pollution. Gave orders for all water to be chlorinated in future.	H.G.hy H.G.hy

Army Form C. 2118.

SANITARY SECTION
XXVII Division
1ST LONDON (CITY OF LONDON) SANITARY C?

WAR DIARY
INTELLIGENCE SUMMARY
(Erase heading not required.)

Instructions regarding War Diaries and Intelligence Summaries are contained in F.S. Regs., Part II. and the Staff Manual respectively. Title pages will be prepared in manuscript.

Place	Date	Hour	Summary of Events and Information	Remarks and references to Appendices
PAS.	5-1-16	9.30 ADMS	10-0 to SOUASTRE. With MO i/c inspected new latrine shelters in 8th EAST LANCS area. Proceeded to St AMAND and made a tour of inspection.	
		2.30	Made analysis of water samples.	#G/y
PAS.	6-1-16	9.30 ADMS	10-0 Inspected Billets in PAS. Advised closure of curtin closets, and arrangement for nail latrines to be made.	
		1.30	Visited Squad at SOUASTRE. Proceeded to HUMBERCAMPS. Inspected new latrine shelters, and Billets requiring repairs.	#G/y
PAS.	7-1-16	9.15 ADMS	10-0 to HUMBERCAMP. With MO i/c 6th BEDS Regt made inspection & advised on new latrine shelters, saw MD i/c 10th LOYAL NORTH LANCS re latrine shelters etc.	#G/y
PAS.	8-1-16	9.30 ADMS. 9.45	Water Squad at SOUASTRE. Proceeded to BIENVILLERS. Took sample from Well. Proceeded to POMMIER & with MO i/c inspected Billets etc of 9th N. STAFFS. REGT & 152 Co. RE. Satisfactory.	
		2.30	Made analysis of water samples.	#G/y

Army Form C. 2118.

SANITARY SECTION.
XXVII Division
1ST LONDON (CITY OF LONDON SANITARY Co)

WAR DIARY
INTELLIGENCE SUMMARY.
(Erase heading not required.)

Instructions regarding War Diaries and Intelligence Summaries are contained in F.S. Regs, Part II. and the Staff Manual respectively. Title pages will be prepared in manuscript.

Place	Date	Hour	Summary of Events and Information	Remarks and references to Appendices
PAS	9-1-16	9.30 A.DMS	10-0 Made analysis of Water samples.	#9by
PAS	10-1-16	9.30 DADMS	10-15 to LA CAUCHIE & with MO%c proceeded to Gunlines of 123 Brigade R.F.A. Found use of dug out almost entirely given up. Living conditions greatly improved. Sanitation satisfactory	#9by
		2-0	Carried out Water analysis	
PAS	11-1-16	9.30 A.DMS	10-0 to ST AMAND With MO%c inspected all Transport lines in area. General conditions good.	#9by
		3-0	Visited DIV. WATER STATION. New road now open. R.E. erecting pump house etc in accordance with scheme of water distribution.	
PAS	12-1-16	9.30 A.DMS	10-0 to BIENVILLERS & with MO's %c inspected all Billets etc of 7th & 9th LEICESTER REGTS. Generally satisfactory. Made recommendations on sanitary measures required to be taken.	#9by
PAS	13-1-16	9-15 A.DMS	10-0 to HENU. Re complaint of foul food men in Billet. Proceeded to BERLES & with MO%c saw Billets of 2nd ESSEX REGT. Satisfactory	#9by

WAR DIARY
INTELLIGENCE SUMMARY.
(Erase heading not required.)

Army Form C. 2118.

Place	Date	Hour	Summary of Events and Information	Remarks and references to Appendices
PAS.	14-1-16	9-15 A.M. 10-0 to HENU. Inspected Horse Lines of 12b Brigade RFA, "B" & "C" Batteries. "B" Billet bad. Advised on work required to be done. Proceeded to GAUDIEMPRE & compared & inspected of sanitary conditions Found Billet, made investigation, & gave orders for measures to be taken.	#Bhy	
PAS.	15-1-16	9.30 A.M. 10-0 Carried out experiments with Thresh Steam Disinfector. Results quite satisfactory. Undergarments taken in middle of 50 blankets, subjected 35 mins. All lice & eggs destroyed & death	#Bhy	
PAS	16-1-16	9.30 A.M. 9-45 Investigated insanitary conditions at DIV. HQS. & had matters put right. 10.15 to TANECHON. Advised O.C. YORKSHIRE DRAGOONS on Billets. Advised O.C. 6th LIVERPOOLS (DETACH.) on measures to take against lice	#Bhy	
PAS.	17-1-16	9.30 A.M. 10-0 to ST AMAND Selected site for Horsfall Destructor. Inspected new R.E. latrines & footbaths. 1.45 to POMMIER Inspected Billets of 1/1. KENT R.G.A. & advised on disinfection required after case of Mumps	#Bhy	

Army Form C. 2118.

WAR DIARY

INTELLIGENCE SUMMARY.
(Erase heading not required.)

Instructions regarding War Diaries and Intelligence Summaries are contained in F. S. Regs., Part II. and the Staff Manual respectively. Title pages will be prepared in manuscript.

F. A. SANITARY SECTION.
XXVII Division
1ST LONDON (CITY OF LONDON) SANITARY Co.

Place	Date	Hour	Summary of Events and Information	Remarks and references to Appendices
PAS.	18.1.16	9.30 ADMS	10.0 to HUMBERCAMPS. Saw new RE latrines and inspected repairs carried out to local Destructor.	
		2.0	to GAUDIEMPRE inspected Billets etc of Supply Section DIV. TRAIN. A.S.C. Very satisfactory.	Sgd.y
PAS	19.1.16	9.30 ADMS	Received instructions to carry out experiments for killing lice by fumigation & made necessary arrangements.	
		10.15	to FONCQUEVILLERS Saw Billets, dug outs etc occupied by 8th EAST LANCS REGT. Satisfactory. Tents being used by fatigue party very dirty condition. Had matters put right forthwith	Sgd.y
		2.0	Continued experiments with fumigation.	
PAS	20.1.16	9.30 ADMS	10.0 to SOUASTRE & then to LAHERLIERE. Inspected Billets etc of "J" Kent Heavy Batt. R.G.A., also Wagon lines of 126 Brig. R.F.A. "D" Battery. Made recommendations	Sgd.y
PAS	21.1.16	9.30 ADMS	10.0 to BIENVILLERS Inspected Billets of 154 Co. R.E. (+Ac) 153 Co. R.E. (1+2 Sec) Satisfactory Also 15th BATT. R.G.A. Men airing required in cottage rooms. Reported this matter	Sgd.y

Army Form C. 2118.

WAR DIARY
INTELLIGENCE SUMMARY.
(Erase heading not required.)

Instructions regarding War Diaries and Intelligence Summaries are contained in F. S. Regs, Part II. and the Staff Manual respectively. Title pages will be prepared in manuscript.

No. 7 SANITARY SECTION
XXVIIth Division
1st LONDON (CITY OF LONDON) SANITARY Co.

Place	Date	Hour	Summary of Events and Information	Remarks and references to Appendices
PAS	22-1-16	9.30 A.D.M.S. 10.30 SOUASTRE Inspected Billets of R.M. Artillery (Detach!), 7th Corps Workshop (A.D.D), 111 Trench Mortar Batty. Satisfactory. Visited Squad at POMMIER.	#9/7
PAS	23-1-16	9.30 A.D.M.S. Instructions re fumigation. 11.30 Visited WATER STATION. new pipe line in course of construction	#9/7
PAS	24-1-16	9.30 A.D.M.S. Experiments with fumigation. Results better. 6.0 Handed over command of Section to Major ADDERLEY (DADMS)	#9/7
PAS	25-1-16	Report of work carried out during absence by N new Horsfall Destructor taken to St AMAND and arrangements made for erection. This for use of Transport Units in village. Water Station visited. Satisfactory. C/E No q Mot. Lab. took sample of water.	#9/7
PAS	26-1-16	Erection of Destructor superintended. Visited Squad at POMMIER re Ablution Places of all units, & re RE Latrines provision of footboards &c. 2.0 pm Reported to A.D.M.S.	#9/7

T2134. Wt. W708—776. 500/000. 4/15. Sir J. C. & S.

Army Form C. 2118.

WAR DIARY
INTELLIGENCE SUMMARY.
(Erase heading not required.)

Instructions regarding War Diaries and Intelligence Summaries are contained in F.S. Regs., Part II. and the Staff Manual respectively. Title pages will be prepared in manuscript.

XXVII Division

Place	Date	Hour	Summary of Events and Information	Remarks and references to Appendices
PAS	27-1-16		Timber drawn for footbaths (RE Laturies) delivered in areas and arrangements made for fixing.	#5/1
PAS	28-1-16		Destructor at ST AMAND finished.	#5/1
PAS	29-1-16		Report on arrangements made in areas by Units for Ablution Places.	#5/1 Finished Report & forwarded to ADMS
PAS	30-1-16		Visited BIENVILLERS. Investigated case of CEREBRO SPINAL FEVER (4th LEICESTER REGT) & had necessary disinfection done. Also investigated case of MEASLES in 13th KINGS ROYAL RIFLE CORPS, & had disinfection carried out	#5/1
PAS	31-1-16		Visited Squad at POMMIER & settled matters	#5/1

Feb.
March } 1916.
April

37th Divol. Sanitary Section.

div:
37th San: Lect

vol 7

Confidential.

War Diary
of
Sanitary Section, 37th Division,

from Feb. 1st 1916 to Feb. 29th 1916

(Volume VII)

H.S.... Capt
RAMC(T)
C/C

Army Form C. 2118.

WAR DIARY
INTELLIGENCE SUMMARY.
(Erase heading not required.)

XXVII Division

Instructions regarding War Diaries and Intelligence Summaries are contained in F. S. Regs., Part II. and the Staff Manual respectively. Title pages will be prepared in manuscript.

Place	Date	Hour	Summary of Events and Information	Remarks and references to Appendices
PAS.	1-2-16	10-0	ADMS. Handed him list of French trench Incinerators in Div Area	
		2-0	Called at Squads. Gave instructions re supervision of Indian Cavalry Corps at LAHERLIERE.	#6hy
PAS.	2-2-16	10-0	Proceeded to BIENVILLERS & took sample of water from subterranean gallery. Called at GAUDIEMPRE. Enquired into offensive smell from village pond. Further enquires to be made.	
		4-0	Reported to ADMS result of analysis on water from BIENVILLERS	#6hy
PAS	3-2-16	10-0	Inspected Billets just taken up in PAS.	
		2-0	Reported to ADMS. supplied particulars & map of wells LAHERLIERE.	
PAS.	4-2-16	9-30	Called on Squad at SOUASTRE, proceeded to LAHERLIERE and reported to MO i/c Indian Cav. Corps. Counted particulars of wells	#6hy
PAS.	5-2-16		O/C Section took over Section from DADMS.	
PAS.	6-2-16	9.30	ADMS. Inspected sundry Billets in PAS.	#6hy
PAS.	7-2-16	9.30	ADMS. Instructions from ADMS re move.	#6hy
		10-15	ADMS to HUMBERCAMPS Advised re disinfection. Proceeded to LAHERLIERE saw MO i/c Indian Cav. Corps.	#6hy

Army Form C. 2118.

WAR DIARY
or
INTELLIGENCE SUMMARY.
(Erase heading not required.)

1st LONDON (CITY OF LONDON) SANITARY CO.

Instructions regarding War Diaries and Intelligence Summaries are contained in F. S. Regs., Part II. and the Staff Manual respectively. Title pages will be prepared in manuscript.

Place	Date	Hour	Summary of Events and Information	Remarks and references to Appendices
PAS	8-2-16	9.30 A.M.	10-D to SOUASTRE, ST AMAND, HUMBERCAMPS, saw NCO i/c on various matters. Proceeded to La BAZEQUE FARM advised on drainage.	#84
PAS	9-2-16	9.30 A.M.	2-D to Squads, SOUASTRE & POMMIER, settled various questions	#84
PAS	10-2-16	9.30 A.M.	Called SOUASTRE, ST AMAND. Saw MO i/c 1st Bde RFA ref. various matters	#84
		2.15 15	BAVINCOURT. Obtained particulars of water supply in new Div area.	#84
PAS	11-2-16	9.30 A.M.	10.30 to BAILLEULMONT & BAILLEUVAL. Made general tour of inspection saw Billets & wells. Noted work required to put villages in sanitary condition #84	#84
PAS	12-2-16	9.30 A.M.	10-15 to BAILLEULMONT & BAILLEUVAL. Left NCO i/c each village. Proceeded to LARBRET & BAVINCOURT. Made tour of inspection & noted wells.	#84
PAS	13-2-16	9.30 A.M.	Proceeded to ST AMAND re new Billets for Squad.	#84
PAS	14-2-16	9.30 A.M.	10-15 to LARBRET, BAILLEULMONT & BAILLEUVAL. Progress made by units satisfactory. Reported ADMS.	#84
PAS	15-2-16	9.30 A.M.	10-15 to WARLINCOURT with MO i/c inspected huts & sanitary arrangements of DIV AMM COLUMN & advised on work still required to be done. Saw Liaison Officer re Billets now at BAVINCOURT.	#84
PAS	16-2-16		2.20 Visited Water Station, WARLINCOURT. Satisfactory	#84

T2134. Wt. W708—776. 500000. 4/15. Sir J. C. & S.

Army Form C. 2118.

WAR DIARY
INTELLIGENCE SUMMARY
(Erase heading not required.)

SANITARY
XXXVII Division
1ST LONDON (CITY OF LONDON) SANITARY C

Instructions regarding War Diaries and Intelligence Summaries are contained in F.S. Regs., Part II. and the Staff Manual respectively. Title pages will be prepared in manuscript.

Place	Date	Hour	Summary of Events and Information	Remarks and references to Appendices
PAS	17-2-16	9.30 ADMS	Squad moved here from SOUASTRE. Called at Squad, POMMIER. Proceeded to BAVINCOURT, supervised clearing up of village & arranged sanitary areas. Inspected and arranged re new Billet for Section. 6.45 Reported to ADMS	#6y
PAS	18-2-16	9.25 NZMD. 10. O AAQMG re distribution of gift Baths 10.30 to ST AMAND, called on 110th Bde.Hqrs. re village bath house. Proceeded to BAVINCOURT, met ADMS & accompanied him on tour of inspection. Sanitary work progressing. Proceeded to BAILLEULMONT & BAILLEULVAL. Progress of work satisfactory	#6y
PAS	19-2-16	9.15 ADMS. 10. O to ST AMAND, called on 110th Bde Hqrs, accompanied Staff Capt. to HUMBERCAMPS re village Bath house. Proceeded to BAVINCOURT and made tour of inspection. A great deal of work remains to be done. Village left in very insanitary condition. Hedges & orchards fouled everywhere with excreta. Refuse & manure everywhere. 6.45 Reported to ADMS	#6y

Army Form C. 2118.

WAR DIARY
INTELLIGENCE SUMMARY.
(Erase heading not required.)

IV xxxvii Division

Place	Date	Hour	Summary of Events and Information	Remarks and references to Appendices
PAS	20.2.16		9.30 ADMS made arrangements for supervising clearing up on evacuation of Hqrs. Units, PAS. 10.30 Proceeded to BAYINCOURT. Tour of inspection with NCO i/charge 11.0 Section left PAS & proceeded to new Hqrs. at BAYINCOURT.	
BAYINCOURT	21.2.16		Supervised work in village. 11.0 Reported ADMS. 2.0 Proceeded to PAS. Made tour of inspection with NCO i/c clearing up. Several billets still require attention. 6.45 Reported to ADMS.	
BAYINCOURT	22.2.16		9.30 ADMS. 10.0 Proceeded to PAS. Made inspection of Billets, all satisfactory. 2.0 Accompanied ADMS to LUCHEUX re sanitation & water supply at 3rd ARMY SCHOOL	
BAYINCOURT	23.2.16		9.30 ADMS. 10.20 to BAILLEULVAL, made tour of inspection with NCO i/c. Progress very good. 2.30 Tour of inspection BAYINCOURT.	
BAYINCOURT	24.2.16		9.30 ADMS. 10.30 BAILLEULMONT, made tour of inspection with NCO i/c. Saw GenL Lorac & advised on disposal of sullage water. 2.30 Tour of inspection BAYINCOURT.	
BAYINCOURT	25.2.16		9.30 ADMS. Supervised work in village.	

Army Form C. 2118.

WAR DIARY
or
INTELLIGENCE SUMMARY.
(Erase heading not required.)

SANITARY SECTION
XXXVII Division

Instructions regarding War Diaries and Intelligence Summaries are contained in F. S. Regs., Part II. and the Staff Manual respectively. Title pages will be prepared in manuscript.

Place	Date	Hour	Summary of Events and Information	Remarks and references to Appendices
BAVINCOURT	26.2.16	9.30	ADMS. Tour of inspection BAVINCOURT.	
		2.30	to LARBRET re Water supply from well at Railway Stn. Proceeded to POMMIER, saw NCO i/c squad on various matters.	
		6.45	Reported to ADMS.	#64
BAVINCOURT	27.2.16	9.30	ADMS Supervised work in village.	#65
BAVINCOURT	28.2.16	9.30	ADMS. 10-0.16 GOUY called on ADMS & DADMS, 55th Div re supervision of this Division's Units in my area.	
		2.30	O/C San. Section, 55th Div. called. Discussed sundry matters re of Ambulance withdrawn owing to state of roads.	#66
BAVINCOURT	29.2.16	9.30	ADMS. 10-0 to GAUDIEMPRE. Made tour of inspection with NCO i/c. A few matters to be attended to.	
		2.30	Tour of inspection BAVINCOURT. 5.20 Reported to ADMS	#67

37th San Sec
Vol 8

Confidential.

War Diary
of
Sanitary Section, 37th Division, B.E.F.

From March 1st 1916 to March 31st 1916

(Volume VIII)

H Gross Capt
RAMC
O/C

COMMITTEE FOR THE
MEDICAL HISTORY OF THE WAR
Date 9 - JUN 1915

WAR DIARY or INTELLIGENCE SUMMARY.

Army Form C. 2118.

31 Division

Place	Date	Hour	Summary of Events and Information	Remarks and references to Appendices
BAVINCOURT	1.3.16	9.30 A.M.	Tour of inspection in village 11-0 to STANAND saw Cpl Y/c re sundry matters	
BAVINCOURT	2.3.16	9.30 A.M.	Inspected area occupied by 1/3rd LANCS. FIELD AMB (55 Div) advised on sanitary matters. 2-0 Visited water supply at LARBRET STATION and made arrangements for cleaning, proceeded to WATER STATION WARLINCOURT. Everything satisfactory.	
BAVINCOURT	3.3.16	9.30 A.M.	Occupied in village all day	
BAVINCOURT	3.3.16	9.30 A.M.	10.20 to L'CAUCHIE re case of Diphtheria (civilian) advised on necessary precautions to be taken. Advised re village Bath House	
BAVINCOURT	5.3.16	9.30 A.M.	10-15 to BAILLEVILMONT & BAILEUVAL, sanitary conditions good. Proceeded to Squad at POMMIER, and settled matters requiring attention	
BAVINCOURT	6.3.16	9.30 A.M.	10-0 to LA HERLIERE, conditions in this village very bad. 2-45 Visited WATER STN., WARLINCOURT. Satisfactory. Proceeded to STANAND saw squad.	

Army Form C. 2118.

SANITARY SECTION
37 Division
1ST LONDON (CITY OF LONDON) SANITARY CO

WAR DIARY
or
INTELLIGENCE SUMMARY.
(Erase heading not required.)

Instructions regarding War Diaries and Intelligence Summaries are contained in F. S. Regs., Part II. and the Staff Manual respectively. Title pages will be prepared in manuscript.

Place	Date	Hour	Summary of Events and Information	Remarks and references to Appendices
BAVINCOURT	7.3.16	9.30 A3md	10.20 to WARLINCOURT & with MO % inspected Billets etc of DIV. TRAIN A.S.C. Advised on improvements to be put in hand	
		1.45 A3md	accompanied him to LUCHEUX. Visited Sanitary Section, H2 Div.	HQy
BAVINCOURT	8.3.16	9.20 A3md	Occupied in village. Arrangements made re village baths	
		2.0 to	LA CAUCHIE, called on Town Mayor re village baths.	HQy
BAVINCOURT	9.3.16	9.30 A3md	9.45 to BAILLEULMONT + with MO/c inspected Billets etc of 123 Bde RFA & 13 RIFLE BDE. Advised on improvements required at once	HQy
BAVINCOURT	10.3.16	9.30 A3md	Field Ambulance reported for duty with us.	
		10.30	Proceeded to LUCHEUX, saw NCO/c Sanitary Section, H2 Div. re working of control in village occupied by Div. Troops.	HQy
BAVINCOURT	11.3.16	9.30 A.M.J	10.30 to LA CAUCHIE, Town Mayor re Baths, promised ⊙ to GAUDIEMPRE & saw Squad re sundry matters.	HQy
BAVINCOURT	12.3.16	9.30 A3md	Warned re mort. 2.0 to LUCHEUX, saw Sanitary Officer, H2 Div. re transfer of control in village.	HQy
BAVINCOURT	13.3.16	9.30 A3md	Instructions received re mort. 10.0 to GAUDIEMPRE, HENU,	

Army Form C. 2118.

WAR DIARY
or
INTELLIGENCE SUMMARY.
(Erase heading not required.)

Instructions regarding War Diaries and Intelligence Summaries are contained in F.S. Regs. Part II. and the Staff Manual respectively. Title pages will be prepared in manuscript.

Place	Date	Hour	Summary of Events and Information	Remarks and references to Appendices
BAVINCOURT	13.3.16 (cont)		BIENVILLERS. Settled sundry matters	#6/
BAVINCOURT	14.3.16	9.30 ADMS	Instructions re mort. Started village Baths, temporarily. Sun Ay Sanitary Section. 10-0 to BAILLEUMONT, BAILLEUVAL, saw Town Majors re sundry matters	#6/
BAVINCOURT	15.3.16	9.30 ADMS	Instructions re mort. Accompanied ADMS to LUCHEUX. Inspected Village re work to be immediately taken in hand. Received orders re mort.	#6/
BAVINCOURT	16.3.16	9.30 ADMS	11.30 to LUCHEUX, saw Sanitary Officer 4th Div. & settled matters re cleaning control in villages. Proceeded to GAUDIEMPRE & saw Squad re sundry matters	#6/
BAVINCOURT	17.3.16	9.30 ADMS	11-0 to GAUDIEMPRE. Saw C/O & MO/c 4th ENTRENCHING BATTy re sundry matters 4-0 Settled squad at POMMIER	#6/
BAVINCOURT	18.3.16	9.45 ADMS	10-15 to BAILLEUMONT & BAILLEUVAL, saw NCO's i/c & gave instructions re cleaning up etc. 6-0 Squad of two NCO's returned from BAILLEUVAL to N.2.D.	#6/

Army Form C. 2118.

37 Divn.

WAR DIARY
or
INTELLIGENCE SUMMARY.
(Erase heading not required.)

Place	Date	Hour	Summary of Events and Information	Remarks and references to Appendices
BAVINCOURT	19.3.16	9.30 a.m.	ADMS. 10.0 Proceeded with advance party to LUCHEUX. Took over Billets for Section. Made tour of village with NCO % advance party & arranged for necessary work to be put in hand.	#Ch
BAVINCOURT	20.3.16	9.0 a.m.	ADMS. 11.0 Section removed to LUCHEUX. Sanitary work in village progressing. A great deal of necessary work to be done.	#Ch
LUCHEUX	21.3.16	9.30 a.m.	ADMS Distribution given to NCOs of Section of duties.	
		10.30	Tour of inspection with DADMS and arrangements made for required labour to be proceeded with. Squads sent out to take charge of outlying villages.	#Ch
LUCHEUX	22.3.16	9.30 a.m.	10.0 Made tour of village with Town Major & supplied for large fatigue party to carry out work.	
		6.30	Reported to ADMS as great amount of work required to be done	#Ch
LUCHEUX	23.3.16	9.30 a.m.	ADMS. 10.0 to WARLUZEL with MO % to LEICESTER REGT. Saw Town Major & made tour of village. Temporary sanitary measures taken, permanent arrangements in hand	
		5.30	Reported progress to ADMS	#Ch

WAR DIARY
or
INTELLIGENCE SUMMARY.
(Erase heading not required.)

Army Form C. 2118.

37 Division

Place	Date	Hour	Summary of Events and Information	Remarks and references to Appendices
LUCHEUX	24-3-16	9.30 ADMS	to NEUVILLETTE saw MO i/c 12 K.R.RIFLES & inspected some of Billets & sanitary areas occupied by Unit. Temporary latrines etc. still in use (Proceeded to BARLY, called on MO i/c 13th R.FUSILIERS. Sanitary measures taken, improvements about.)	#2/
		5.30	Reported progress to ADMS	
LUCHEUX	25-3-16	9.30 ADMS	9.45 to PAS Inspected Camp to be occupied by Div'n R.F.A. and advised on sanitary requirements	
		6.0 ADMS	Reported at RFA Camp, work required & labour necessary. #2/	
LUCHEUX	26-3-16	9.30 ADMS	Made tour of village.	
LUCHEUX	27-3-16	9.30 ADMS	10.30 to SOS ST LEGER & with MO i/c 6th LEICESTER REGT inspected all Billets & sanitary areas of Unit. Progress good.	
		2.0 to SOS ST LEGER & with MO i/c 7th LEICESTER REGT inspected all sanitary areas & Billets. Advised on matters requiring attention		
		6.0 ADMS	Reported progress. 7.30 AA&QMG re labour for RE Camp #2/	
LUCHEUX	28-3-16	8.45 ADMS	9.0 to R.E. Camp, PAS. Took two NCO's to take charge of sanitary work. Supervised work & made all necessary arrangements for large fatigue for work at RE Camp. #2/	

Army Form C. 2118.

WAR DIARY
or
INTELLIGENCE SUMMARY.
(Erase heading not required.)

xxxvii Summary

Instructions regarding War Diaries and Intelligence Summaries are contained in F. S. Regs., Part II. and the Staff Manual respectively. Title pages will be prepared in manuscript.

Place	Date	Hour	Summary of Events and Information	Remarks and references to Appendices
LUCHEUX	29.2.16	9-0 A.M.	Inspection made in village	A57
LUCHEUX	30.2.16	9-0 A.M.	Advised re Bath House, arrangements made to carry out necessary change. 10-30 to R.A. Camp. Work progressing slowly	
		7-15 A.M.	Report progress	reply
LUCHEUX	31.2.16	9-0 A.M.	to St AMAND saw Sanitary Officer 4th Div. re transfer of control of thirts outside area of 37th Div. Proceeded to HUMBERCAMPS, saw Squad & gave orders for their trek down to H.qrs 4th Div	

T2134. Wt. W708—776. 500000. 4/15. Sir J. C. & S.

37 Sanitary Vol 9

Confidential.

"War Diary"
of
Sanitary Section, 37th Division
from April 1st 1916 to April 30th 1916.

(Volume IX) O.C.

H Gray Capt
RAMC

Army Form C. 2118.

WAR DIARY
INTELLIGENCE SUMMARY
(Erase heading not required.)

Instructions regarding War Diaries and Intelligence Summaries are contained in F. S. Regs., Part II. and the Staff Manual respectively. Title Pages will be prepared in manuscript.

Place	Date	Hour	Summary of Events and Information	Remarks and references to Appendices
LUCHEUX	1.4.16	9.0 A.D.M.S.	Inspected Hqrs. Bath House, not yet ready.	
		10.45 to OCCOCHES	with M.O/c inspected Billets etc. of 9 N. STAFFS REGT. general conditions very fair.	
		2.30 to R.A. Camp, MONDICOURT. Inspected sanitary arrangements		
			moved plan owing to shortage of labour. 4.15 A.D.M.S.	
LUCHEUX	2.4.16	9.0 A.D.M.S.	Tour of village.	H.Q.H.
LUCHEUX	3.4.16	9.0 A.D.M.S. 10.30 to DOULLENS, with M.O/c inspected Billets etc of Div. Supply Column. Reported on dirty condition of some Billets.		H.Q.H.
		3.15 A.D.M.S		
LUCHEUX	4.4.16	9.0 A.D.M.S. accompanied him on visit to ST.POL.		
		2.0 Visited HQR BATHS not yet complete		
		3.30 to R.A.Camp, MONDICOURT, Brigade arriving, work nearly complete. H.Q.H.		
LUCHEUX	5.4.16	9.0 A.D.M.S. 10.0 to BREVILLERS. Tour of inspection of Billets of 4/5th		
		9 LEICESTER REGT. Satisfactory.		
LUCHEUX	6.4.16	9.0 A.D.M.S. 10.0 to MEZEROLLES, with M.O/c inspected Billets etc of		
		10 R. FUSILIERS. Billets & surroundings very dirty & insanitary.		
		Reported thereon. Proceeded to BARLY with M.O/c inspected		
		Billets etc of 13 R. FUSILIERS. Conditions very fair. Met A.D.M.S		H.Q.H.
		2xw to Hours met him.		
LUCHEUX	7.4.16	9.0 A.D.M.S. 10.0 to GROUCHES. Made tour of village & inspected Billets		
		etc of 1/4 B.W. RFA Room for improvement in sanitation		H.Q.H.
		4.45 A.D.M.S.		

Army Form C. 2118.

WAR DIARY
INTELLIGENCE SUMMARY

(Erase heading not required.)

Instructions regarding War Diaries and Intelligence Summaries are contained in F. S. Regs., Part II. and the Staff Manual respectively. Title Pages will be prepared in manuscript.

Place	Date	Hour	Summary of Events and Information	Remarks and references to Appendices
LUCHEUX	8-4-16	9.0 A Dm D	9.20 Inspection of village with N.C.O %c.	#94
LUCHEUX	9-4-16	9.0 A Dm D	Visited Hqr. Baths. 2.30 ADmD re distribution of section	#94
LUCHEUX	10-4-16	9.0 ADmD	10.15 to BREVILLERS, with MO %c inspected Billets etc. of DN.TRAIN. No. 144 Coys. Arrived on required improvements. Inspected Billets etc. section of BRIDGEING TRAIN. Billets duty reported. 2.15 Inspected front of LUCHEUX.	#94 #94
LUCHEUX	11-4-16	9.0 ADmD	Section re-called to Hqrs. for training etc.	#94
LUCHEUX	12-4-16	9.0 ADmD	Training of Section	#94
LUCHEUX	13-4-16	9.0 ADmD 2.30	Training of section. Trial mobilization. Ready for road 1½ hrs.	#94
LUCHEUX	14-4-16	9.0 ADmD 11.0	Training of Section. Called on O/C 8th Div on ration R.F.C. & advised on necessary sanitary measures required to be taken	#94
LUCHEUX	15-4-16	9.0 ADmD 2.30	Training of Section to GROUCHES. Condition of village now satisfactory	#94 #94
LUCHEUX	16-4-16	9.0 ADmD	Inspected sundry billets in village.	#94
LUCHEUX	17-4-16	9.0 ADmD	10.0 to R.A. Camp, MONDICOURT. With MO %c inspected area occupied by 126 Bde. Dny train. Inspected area of 125 Bde. & arrangements for storage of meat. Cookhouses dirty, had arrangements for storage of meat. Inspected area of 124 Bde with MO %c. Condition very fair.	#94
~~LUCHEUX~~ LUCHEUX	19-4-16	8.30 ADmD	10.15 to WARLUZEL, with M.D.%c inspected Billets etc. of 10 L.NORTH. LANCS. REGT. Condition very good.	#94 #94

Army Form C. 2118.

WAR DIARY
or
INTELLIGENCE SUMMARY
(Erase heading not required.)

Instructions regarding War Diaries and Intelligence Summaries are contained in F. S. Regs., Part II. and the Staff Manual respectively. Title Pages will be prepared in manuscript.

Place	Date	Hour	Summary of Events and Information	Remarks and references to Appendices
LUCHEUX	19-4-16		6.30 ADMS 10.45 to BEAUREPAIRE FME. Inspected area occupied by YORKS. DRAGOONS. Made recommendations. Proceeded to HALLOY. Inspected area around HUT CAMP. Foul areas left by previous troops to be cleaned. Reported to ADMS.	HGA
LUCHEUX	20-4-16		8.30 ADMS 10.0 to NEUVILLETTE Inspected portion of village with M.O/c. a few foul areas requiring attention. Saw Bath House, Boothams. 2.30 to HALLOY. Fatigue party sent to clean up & prepare for incoming troops. Gave instructions for necessary work	HGA
LUCHEUX	21-4-16		8.30 ADMS re Baths available in village 9.45 to SUS ST LEGER Tour of inspection in area occupied by 6th BEDFS. REGT. General condition good. 2.15 Accompanied ADMS to NEZEROLLES re cases of Measles.	HGA
LUCHEUX	22-4-16		8.30 ADMS Bath House re drainage system. Tour of inspection village.	HGA
LUCHEUX	23-4-16		9.0 ADMS. Inspection of Baths with ADMS. 2.30 to HALLOY. Inspected Hut Camp. Matters requiring attention Reported thereon.	HGA
LUCHEUX	24-4-16		8.30 ADMS 9.45 to SUS ST LEGER & with MO/c inspected Billets etc of 8 EAST LANCS REGT. Reported on improvements required.	HGA
LUCHEUX	25-4-16		8.30 ADMS. 10.0 to LE SOUICH with MO/c inspected Billets etc of 11 ROY. WARWICKS. Conditions very good	HGA

Army Form C. 2118.

WAR DIARY
or
INTELLIGENCE SUMMARY
(Erase heading not required.)

Instructions regarding War Diaries and Intelligence Summaries are contained in F.S. Regs., Part II. and the Staff Manual respectively. Title Pages will be prepared in manuscript.

Place	Date	Hour	Summary of Events and Information	Remarks and references to Appendices
LUCHEUX	26.4.16		8.45 ADMO 10.15 to GROUCHES with MO/c inspected Billets etc of 123 BDE. RFA. conditions fair. No bathing arrangements.	HSY
LUCHEUX	27.4.16		9.0 ADMS Inspections in village.	HSY
LUCHEUX	28.4.16		8.30 ADMS. 10.30 to GROUCHES, arranged for Shower Bath installation. Motored to HAUDY, inspected Huts. Still in need of attention.	HSY
LUCHEUX	29.4.16		8.45 2 ADMS. 9.50 to GRENAS with MO/c inspected Billets etc of 37. DIV AMM. COL. Very fair. 2.30 to GROUCHES re Baths.	HSY
LUCHEUX	30.4.16		9.0 DADMS. Orders received re move. Outside Sqnads visited HDrs. gave them instructions. Their work.	HSY

Jan
37 San Sec
Vol II

Confidential.

War Diary

of

Sanitary Section,
37th Division.
B. E. F.

from :- June 1st 1916 to June 30th 1916

(Volumn XI)

H Smey Capt
RAMC (T.F.)
O/C

COMMITTEE ... THE
MEDICAL HISTORY OF THE WAR
Date

Army Form C. 2118.

WAR DIARY
INTELLIGENCE SUMMARY
(Erase heading not required.)

SANITARY SECTION.
XXVIII Divn.
1st LONDON (CITY OF LONDON) SANITARY Co.

Instructions regarding War Diaries and Intelligence Summaries are contained in F. S. Regs., Part II. and the Staff Manual respectively. Title Pages will be prepared in manuscript.

Place	Date	Hour	Summary of Events and Information	Remarks and references to Appendices
BAVINCOURT	1.6.16	8.30	ADMS 10.0 to COULLEMONT. Inspected village, condition good	HQly
BAVINCOURT	2.6.16	8.30	ADMS 9.0 with ADMS to BIENVILLERS. With N.C.O./c village. Inspected various areas. Made enquiries re suspected case of Diphtheria	HQly
		2.30	Gave Lecture on Sanitation to Cooking Class	
BAVINCOURT	3.6.16	8.30	ADMS. 9.15 to LA CAUCHIE. Inspected Baths, very satisfactory	HQly
		10.0	with M.O./c inspected area at BAVINCOURT occupied by 1/9R LEICESTERS also areas of sundry small units. General condition great	
		2.30	With M.O/c inspected area occupied by D.N. TRAIN. Satisfactory	HQly
BAVINCOURT	4.6.16	8.30	ADMS. Visited AA+DMG re wells & Sanitation in trenches	
		11.30	With N.C.O./c village. made inspections at LARBRET. Gave orders re cleaning up. required	
BAVINCOURT	5.6.16	8.30	ADMS / 9.45 to BERLES. Made inspections with MO i/c 10RT FUSILIERS and 9TH STAFFS. Inspected special well, and took samples for testing	HQly
		2.30	Inspected Transport lines in BAVINCOURT and advised on improvements	HQly
BAVINCOURT	6.6.16	8.30	ADMS 10.15 to BIENVILLERS. Inspected water system, level of area of 101 Bde RGA. Took particulars of RE Labour Covers re cost.	HQly
			Visit to F.A. Govr board system	
BAVINCOURT	7.6.16	8.30	ADMS - General duties	
BAVINCOURT	8.6.16	8.30	ADMS. Inspection of field sanitary appliances got together. Inspected by DADMS & a DH+DMS.	HQly
		2.30	Lecture on Cookhouse Sanitation to Cooking Class	
BAVINCOURT	9.6.16	8.30	ADMS. General duties	HQly
BAVINCOURT	10.6.16	8.30	ADMS. 10.0 to SAVY, with MO/c. Move inspected area occupied by 1D. LOAN NORTH-ANCS. Advised re improvements required.	HQly

2449 Wt. W14957/M90 750,000 1/16 J.B.C. & A. Forms/C.2118/12.

Army Form C. 2118.

SANITARY SECTION.
1ST LONDON (CITY OF LONDON) XXXVII Division

WAR DIARY
or
INTELLIGENCE SUMMARY
(Erase heading not required.)

Instructions regarding War Diaries and Intelligence Summaries are contained in F. S. Regs., Part II. and the Staff Manual respectively. Title Pages will be prepared in manuscript.

Place	Date	Hour	Summary of Events and Information	Remarks and references to Appendices
BAVINCOURT	11-6-16	8.30 ADMS	General duties	#94
BAVINCOURT	12-6-16	8.30 ADMS 10-0 to SAULTY	Inspection with NCO i/c village. A.S.I.F. MO i/c inspected area of Div. Amm. Column. Generally satisfactory	#94 #94
BAVINCOURT	13-6-16	8.30 ADMS 10-0 to BAILLEULVAL	Investigated cases of diphtheria & advised on necessary precautions to be taken. With MO i/c inspected area of 13 Roy Fusiliers. Satisfactory. Proceeded to BAILLEULVAL, advised MO i/c 1st BEDFORDS on sanitary matters	#94 #94
BAVINCOURT	14-6-16	8.30 ADMS 2.30	Inspections in village. Gave lecture Bootchown sanitation to Cooks & Class. Handed over command of Unit to Capt Breen, D.A.D.M.S. previous to proceeding on leave	#94 July
BAVINCOURT	15-6-16		Summary of Report from NCO i/c Section as follows: Laboratory Coy'l made further test of special Will et BERLES Room for fumigation added by Town Major. Receipt of fumigation apparatus & village pail in hand	#94
BAVINCOURT	16-6-16		Visited COULLEMENT saw Town Major & Co. in village & removal of manure. Visited SAULTY on manure question. Changed fitting up of fumigation chamber	#94
BAVINCOURT	17-6-16		Proceeded to SAULTY on manure question. Work proceeding on fumigation chamber	#94
BAVINCOURT	18-6-16		Cleared out settling tank & filter bed, village baths. Fumigation chamber completed	#94
BAVINCOURT	19-6-16		Inspected with NCO i/c Northern portion of village area & infantry camp	#94

WAR DIARY
INTELLIGENCE SUMMARY

(Erase heading not required.)

Army Form C. 2118.

SANITARY SECTION.
1ST [CANADIAN?] SANITARY CO.

Place	Date	Hour	Summary of Events and Information	Remarks and references to Appendices
BAVINCOURT	20-6-16		Inspect of DIV. HQRS attended IG., made arrangements re manure heap near Combatant.	#66
BAVINCOURT	21-6-16		Inspection with DADMS of M.M.POLICE Billets etc, condition reported to DADM. Sunday work carried out.	#67
BAVINCOURT	22-6-16		Visited VII Corps Workshops (SAULTY) re Latrines & Dinner accommodation. Visited COUTURELLE re removal of manure. Work progressing.	#64
BAVINCOURT	23-6-16		Sunday work carried out	#64
BAVINCOURT	24-6-16	12-0	Took over command of Section.	#65
BAVIN COURT	25-6-16	9-0 ADMS	Tour of village re manure dumping	#66
BAVINCOURT	26-6-16	8-30 ADMS	General duties.	#67
BAVINCOURT	27-6-16	8-30 ADMS 10-0	Go SAULTY with MO/c 1st LEICESTERS inspected area of Unit. Condition very fair	#66
BAVINCOURT	28-6-16	8-30 ADMS 10-0	Go BAILLEULMONT saw MO/c 123 Bde.RFA. re conditions at Wagon Lines, BAVINCOURT, & re remedial. Condition of village fair.	#67
BAVINCOURT	29-6-16	8-30 ADMS 10-30	LAHERLIERE Tour of inspection. General conditions greatly improved.	#67
BAVINCOURT	30-6-16	8-30 ADMS. 10-0	COULLEMONT Inspected areas of DIV. SUPPLY COLUMN, & "B" Echelon DIV. AMM. COLUMN. Former in good condition, advised improvements for latter.	#67

37 San Sec
Vol 10

Confidential

War Diary

of

Sanitary Section, 37th Division,

from May 1st 1916 to May 31st 1916

(Volume X)

O/C H Gross Capt
RAMC

WAR DIARY
INTELLIGENCE SUMMARY

(Erase heading not required.)

Army Form C. 2118.

SANITARY SECTION
xxvii Division
1st LONDON (CITY OF LONDON) SANITARY Co.

Place	Date	Hour	Summary of Events and Information	Remarks and references to Appendices
LUCHEUX	1-5-16	9.0	DADMS. 10.30 Made tour of 110th Infy. Brigade area. Units re measures to be taken to have area in sanitary condition.	#94/1
		5.30	Visited GROUCHES re Shower Baths. Working excellently.	#94/1
LUCHEUX	2-5-16	9.0	DADMS 9.45 to BAVINCOURT. Tour of inspection, noted work required to put in hand.	#94/1
LUCHEUX	3-5-16	9.0	Section proceeded to BAVINCOURT	
		12.30	Section arrived at BAVINCOURT & took up Billets	#94/1
BAVINCOURT	4-5-16	8.45	ADMS. N.C.O's sent out to inspect & report on state of all villages in area. Inspected & made necessary arrangements in BAVINCOURT	#94/1
BAVINCOURT	5-5-16	8.45	DDMS. N.C.O's sent out to inspect area & report on bathing arrangements. Necessary work in village progressing.	#94/1
		4.30	to SAULTY re Baths, arranged to have billows Butchfixed up. Made tour of village.	
BAVINCOURT	6-5-16	9.0	ADMS. 10.15 with DDMS to LARBRET re water supply for Ambulance Champs	#94/1
		2.30	to SAULTY, COULLEMONT, COUTURELLE and WARLUZEL. Tour of each village. Condition very fair.	#94/1
BAVINCOURT	7-5-16	9.0	DADMS 11.0 inspected village with town major. Arranged distribution of section	#94/1 #94/1

Army Form C. 2118.

WAR DIARY
or
INTELLIGENCE SUMMARY
(Erase heading not required.)

SANITARY SECTION.
1ST LONDON (CITY OF LONDON) SANITARY Co.

Instructions regarding War Diaries and Intelligence Summaries are contained in F. S. Regs., Part II. and the Staff Manual respectively. Title Pages will be prepared in manuscript.

Place	Date	Hour	Summary of Events and Information	Remarks and references to Appendices
BAVINCOURT	9.5.16	8.20	ADMS 10.0 with ADMS to BIENVILLERS and HANNESCAMPS. Tour of inspection. A great deal of cleaning up to done. Distilled Section over area	
BAVINCOURT	9.5.16	5.30	Inspected & advised on sanitation of Rifling Points	
		6.30	ADMS. Informed work in village	
BAVINCOURT	10.5.16	2.30	to LARBRET, COUTURELLE, COULLEMONT re Bath Houses.	
		6.30	ADMS	
BAVINCOURT	11.5.16	10.30	to LAHERLIERE. Saw Town Mayor re Bath House	
		4.30	to COUTURELLE Saw Town Mayor re Baths for village	
		8.30	ADMS 10.0 to BAILLEULVAL. With MOYC inspected areas of limits in village.	
BAVINCOURT	12.5.16	8.30	ADMS 10.0 to LACAUCHIE Saw Town Mayor re starting Baths	
			Saw Town Mayor re Bath House, made inspection of area of factory	
BAVINCOURT	13.5.16	8.45	ADMS. Arranged for drainage pits, Hop Baths.	
			Section to N.C.O on daily visit.	
		6.0	with ADMS to Rifling Points. Inspected Baths at LARBRET. Accommodation insufficient	
BAVINCOURT	14.5.16	8.45	ADMS Tour of village with Corpl in charge.	
BAVINCOURT	15.5.16	8.15	ADMS 10.0 to WARLUZEL Tour of inspection with Corpl in charge arranged with Town Mayor for necessary cleaning up of area	
BAVINCOURT	16.5.16	8.30	ADMS 10.15 to BIENVILLERS. Made inspection of village. Saw Staff Capt 110th Bde re improvement of drainage at Laviolette	

WAR DIARY or INTELLIGENCE SUMMARY

Army Form C. 2118.

SANITARY SECTION, XXVII Division
1ST LONDON (CITY OF LONDON) SANITARY Cº

Place	Date	Hour	Summary of Events and Information	Remarks and references to Appendices
BAVINCOURT	17-5-16	8.30 ADMS	Inspection of village with Coopt in charge	
		2.30 Lecture to Cook's School of Instruction		
		5.0 To SAULTY. Saw CO G 10 L/NORTH LANCS re Bathing arrangements	#Bh	
BAVINCOURT	19-5-16	8.30 X Bind 10.0 To SAULTY & with MO/c 10 LOYAL NORTH LANCS REGT inspected billets and sanitary area of Units in village. Satisfactory	#Bh	
		5.0 Visited CALVAIRE LOUISON re water supply	#Bh	
BAVINCOURT	19-5-16	8.30 ADMS 9.45 To BIENVILLERS re water supplies. Saw NCO i/c village re sanitary matters.		
BAVINCOURT	20-5-16	8.30 ADMS 10-0 To BERLES, inspected well for A.A. Q.M.G. with MO/c inspected Billets etc. of 9 NORTH STAFFS. Very satisfactory	#Bh	
BAVINCOURT	21-5-16	8.45 ADMS Inspections made in village	#Bh	
BAVINCOURT	22-5-16	8.30 ADMS 2.0 To BAILLEULMONT. Saw Coopt i/c on sundry matters. Proceeded to BAILLEULVAL, inspected well near trenches for sample for analysis.	MOh	
BAVINCOURT	23-5-16	8.30 ADMS 10-0 To BAILLEULMONT with MO/c 4 BEDFORDS REGT inspected billets etc. Satisfactory	#Bh	
BAVINCOURT	24-5-16	8.45 ADMS Tour of village with Coopt in charge	#Bh	
BAVINCOURT	25-5-16	9.0 ADMS 10.15 To LARBRET. Made inspection with Coopt i/charge 5.30 with ADMS to SAULTY. Inspected B. Houses & sanitary area of VII Corps Workshops	#Bh	

Army Form C. 2118.

WAR DIARY
or
INTELLIGENCE SUMMARY
(Erase heading not required.)

SANITARY SECTION.
1ST LONDON (CITY OF LONDON) SANITARY Cº

Place	Date	Hour	Summary of Events and Information	Remarks and references to Appendices
BAVINCOURT	26·5·16	8.45 A.D.M.S	10·0 LATTHERLIERE. Made inspection with Lt. Coyl I/charge village	
		2·30	Lecture Sanitation in Cookhouse to Cooks Class	
BAVINCOURT	27·5·16	8·45 A.D.M.S	9·45 LA CAUCHIE Inspection with Lt. Coyl I/charge. With	
			M.O/c 8th LEICESTER REGT Inspected area occupied by Unit	
BAVINCOURT	28·5·16	8·45 A.D.M.S	Instructions in village	
		3·15 A.D.M.S	Discussed Sanitary arrangements in Divnl. Area.	
BAVINCOURT	29·5·16	8·30 A.D.M.S. 10·15	10·15 PAS. Conference with D.A.D.M.S (Sanitation) III Army	
		at Office of D.D.M.S. XII Corps.		
BAVINCOURT	30·5·16	8·30 A.D.M.S	10·15 to LA CAUCHIE With M.O/c 12th Bde. R.F.A. inspected area	
			of Unit. Very fair. Saw Town Major and arranged for	
			Installation of Shower Baths	
		5·0 to SAULTY.	Town of village. General condition good	
BAVINCOURT	31·5·16	9·30 A.D.M.S	Improved work in village	

Confidential.

War Diary

of

Sanitary Section, 37th Division, B.E.F.

from July 1st 1916 to July 31st 1916

(Volume XII)

Army Form C. 2118.

WAR DIARY or INTELLIGENCE SUMMARY

(Erase heading not required.)

SANITARY SECTION.
1ST LONDON (CITY OF LONDON) SANITARY Cº

Instructions regarding War Diaries and Intelligence Summaries are contained in F. S. Regs., Part II. and the Staff Manual respectively. Title Pages will be prepared in manuscript.

Place	Date	Hour	Summary of Events and Information	Remarks and references to Appendices
BAVINCOURT	1-7-16	8.30	ADMO 9.45 with NCO/c Tour of inspection of half village. Areas occupied by RFA Wagon Line in bad condition. Reported to M. O/c	
		11.0	Central to Gouy Eclus (Conference sanitation)	#96
BAVINCOURT	2-7-16	9.0	ASMO. H.O. Warning re move from area. Had equipment packed & made necessary arrangements	#96
BAVINCOURT	3-7-16	8.30	ADMO. Received instructions re move	
		10.0	to BAILLEUVAL saw NCO/c & Town Major re condition of village. Satisfactory. Proceeded to BAILLEUMONT saw NCO/c re clearing up village refuse & burying.	#96
BAVINCOURT	4-7-16	8.30	ADMO. Tour of village	
		5.30	Section proceeded to PAS. 9.30 Proceeded to PAS	
PAS	4-7-16	11.0	Arrived at PAS. Made arrangements for necessary sanitary work to be put in hand.	#96
PAS	5-7-16	8.30	ADMO. Work in village	
		5.0	to MONDICOURT saw Town Major re cleaning up of village.	#96
PAS	6-7-16	8.30	ADMO 10.0 to HUMBERCAMP. Town in indifferent state of cleanliness. Town Major. Enormous amount of cleaning up to be done. Proceeded to HUMBERCOURT, nearly empty. Condition good.	
		3.15	to HQRS. DIV. TRAIN re limber for use from available	#96
PAS	7-7-16	8.30	ADMO. Work in village & general duties.	
			One squad proceeded to WARLINCOURT for duty in area.	#96
PAS	8-7-16	8.30	ADMO Tour of village with DADMS. Arranged for hire of civilian cart. Squad proceeded to MONDICOURT, HENIBERCAMP, POMMIER for duty in area.	
		3.0	POMMIER saw NCO/c Village. Left very dirty	#96

WAR DIARY or INTELLIGENCE SUMMARY

Army Form C. 2118.

SANITARY SECTION.
1ST LONDON SANITARY CO. XXVII (?) SAN SEC.

Place	Date	Hour	Summary of Events and Information	Remarks and references to Appendices
PAS	9-7-16	9.0 ADMD	General duties	#89
PAS	10-7-16	8.30 ADMD. 10.0 to MONDICOURT. Saw M.O/c 8 LINCOLN REGT re methods of sanitation in area.		#89
PAS	11-7-16	8.30 ADMD. 9.45 to HUMBER CAMPS with M.O/c, inspected area of 24th NORTH AND FUSILIERS. Good progress being made. Entire ne kitchens to NCO/c village. Proceeded to GAUDIEMPRE. Saw Town Major re cleaning up of area	#89
PAS	12-7-16	8.30 ADMD. 11.0 to HALLOY. Saw Town Major re cleaning of area & arranged to give assistance	#89
PAS	13-7-16	8.30 ADMD. 9.45 to WARLINCOURT, with M O/c. Very satisfactory. Inspected area of DN AMM. COLUMN, work progressing. Saw M.O/c re removal of manure RTA / Camp being carried up by special fatigue party.	#89
PAS	14-7-16	5.30 ADMD. 9.45 to GAUDIEMPRE, HUMBERCAMP, POMMIER and BIENVILLERS. Saw N.C.D/c re satisfactory cleaning up of villages by limits before leaving. 6.0 Onward squads returned to Section Hqrs. Escorts attached men returned to Battalions	#89
PAS	15-7-16	8.15 ADMD. Instructions re move 11.0 Sent "P.B" men sent to Camp Commandant VII Corps. 2.0 Left PAS 7-15 Arrived GIVENCHY LE-NOBLE	#89
GIVENCHY-LE-NOBLE	16-7-16	8.30 ADMD. Orders re move 10.45 Proceeded to BRYAS Arrive 11.4.30 5-2 Tour of village with BADAIS, necessary arrangements made	#89

WAR DIARY or INTELLIGENCE SUMMARY

Army Form C. 2118.

SANITARY SECTION.
1ST CORPS XXXVII DIVISION SANITARY CO

Place	Date	Hour	Summary of Events and Information	Remarks and references to Appendices
BRYAS	17.7.16	8.30 ADMS	Squads of 3 N.C.Os sent out to work in areas alld to 3 Field Ambces. Inspections in village.	#94
		3.0	To OSTREVILLE, ORLENCOURT, MONCHY-BRETON, BAILLEULVAL-CORNAILLES MARQUAY. Saw MO's i/c units re sanitation in areas & water supply etc.	#94
		7.0 ADMJ		
BRYAS	18.7.16	8.30 ADMS	Instructions re move. Inspections in village.	#94
BRYAS	19.7.16	8.30 ADMS	Instructions re move.	
		10.15	To LA COMTÉ. Saw San. Officer 2nd DIVISION re Sanitation & water supplies in new area.	#94
		6.0 ADMJ		
BRYAS	20.7.16	8.30 ADMS	Orders re move. Tour of village re units clearing up.	
		9.30	Section proceeded to LA COMTÉ.	
		9.30	Left for LA COMTÉ. 10.30 Inspection of Sanitary arrangements at our DIV. HQRS & in village.	#94
		3.0	Tour of village with DADMS.	
LA COMTÉ	21.7.16	8.30 ADMS	10.0 to DIVISION. Inspected with MO's areas occupied by 20, 21, 22, 23 NORTHUMBERLAND FUSILIERS. Sanitary work well in hand. Conditions very fair.	#94
		5.0 ADMJ		
LA COMTÉ	22.7.16	8.45 ADMS	Inspection of village with N.C.O. i/c. Great shortage of men for fatigue work in village.	
		2.0 with DADMS	to ESTRÉE-CAUCHIE, MESNIL-BOUCHÉ with MO i/c at inspection of areas of 10th YORKS & LANCS REGT & 4th MIDDLESEX. Great dearth of men for sanitary work.	#94
		7.0 ADMJ		

Army Form C. 2118.

WAR DIARY
or
INTELLIGENCE SUMMARY
(Erase heading not required.)

SANITARY SECTION.
XXVII
1st LONDON (CITY OF LONDON) SANITARY CO

Place	Date	Hour	Summary of Events and Information	Remarks and references to Appendices
LA COMTÉ	23.7.16	8.45 ADMS.	Inspections in village	AGh
		1.30	To MONDICOURT for Stores	
LA COMTÉ	24.7.16	8.45 ADMS. Orders to move		AGh
		10.15	To CAMBLAIN L'ABBÉ. Saw San. Officer 47th Division re Sanitation & water supplies in new area. Very satisfactory information received.	AGh
		7.15 ADMS. Instructions re move		
LA COMTÉ	25.7.16	8.45 ADMS. 9.0 Inspection with NCO/c at Div. HQRS. Satisfactory Arranged for Method of manure		AGh
		3.0	Divisional Squad at Division re supervising evacuation of Battalions by	
LA COMTÉ	26.7.16	8.45 ADMS. 10.0 to CAMBLAIN L'ABBÉ. arranged with SAN. OFFICER 47 DIV. re Sections changing over re Stores to hand over		AGh
		6.30 ADMS. re billet		
LA COMTÉ CAMBLAIN L'ABBÉ	27.7.16	8.45 ADMS. 8.50 Proceeded to CAMBLAIN L'ABBÉ. 11.30 Arrived. Arranged Billets, Stores etc. Inspected sanitary arrangements of village		AGh
CAMBLAIN L'ABBÉ	28.7.16	8.45 Tour of village with NCO/c Put necessary workmen in hand. Condition of village bad. Advised for men to carry on with 11.20 DDMS IV Corps called. Gave instructions re Sanitation in village & trenches 12.15 Reported to DADMS		AGh
CAMBLAIN L'ABBÉ	29.7.16	8.30 ADMS. Tour of village Work progressing 3.0 Accompanied DADMS to VILLERS AU BOIS and CARENCY. Toured villages saw MO/c 1st NORTHUMBD FUSILIERS & inspected sanitary area of Unit. Agreed Sent off works necessary		AGh

2449 Wt. W14957/M90 750,000 1/16 J.B.C. & A. Forms/C.2118/12.

Army Form C. 2118.

WAR DIARY
or
INTELLIGENCE SUMMARY

(Erase heading not required.)

SANITARY SECTION,
1ST LONDON (CITY OF LONDON) SANITARY Co.

Instructions regarding War Diaries and Intelligence Summaries are contained in F.S. Regs., Part II. and the Staff Manual respectively. Title Pages will be prepared in manuscript.

Place	Date	Hour	Summary of Events and Information	Remarks and references to Appendices
CAMBLAIN L'ABBÉ	30-7-16	8.45	ADMS. With ADMS settled arrangements for carrying out work	
			adt Div. Hqrs.	
			General duties	
CAMBLAIN L'ABBÉ	31-7-16	8.30	ADMS	
		9.15	Inspected village. A large amount of work still necessary	
		11.30	Accompanied ADMS on inspections in village.	

H Simon Capt
RAMC TF

C/O

37th Div
Confidential

War Diary
of
Sanitary Section 37 Division

from Aug. 1st 1916 to Aug 31st 1916

(Volume XIII)

37
(37) San Sec
Vol 13

M

Aug. 1916.

WAR DIARY
or
INTELLIGENCE SUMMARY

(Erase heading not required.)

Army Form C. 2118.

SANITARY SECTION,
XXVII. 2nd/VII
1ST LONDON (CITY OF LONDON) SANITARY Cᵒ.

Place	Date	Hour	Summary of Events and Information	Remarks and references to Appendices
~~Essex~~ CAMBLAIN L'ABBE	1-8-16	6.30 HdQrs	Inspected sanitation at TRA.HqrS & advised thereon. Saw Liaison Officer re civilians removing manure from their yards.	
		9-0		
		10-0	VILLERS-AU-BOIS. Saw Staff Sgt. Le Bele (Infy) re supply of disinfectants called Gov. Servins. Saw T. Major re work required in village.	
			Proceeded to ESTREE-CAUCHIE. Saw T. Major re work required in village, accompanied him on inspection. Enquired into two cases of heads & gave instructions re necessary disinfection. Arranged for N.C.O. to be attached to T.M.O. staff.	
		5.15	Saw HdQrs re fatigue parties.	JBy
CAMBLAIN L'ABBE	2-8-16	8.30 HdQrs.		
		10-0	Saw Sanitary Officer, 9 Div. called. Arranged which areas to supervise.	
		2-0	With DADMS to Gov. Servins. Made inspections in village conditions very poor. Saw T. Major re sundry matters.	JBy
CAMBLAIN L'ABBE	3-8-16	8.30 HdQrs.		
		10.15	to GAUCHIN-LEGAL with M.O/c village, inspected areas of 124 RFA (2 Bdr. Btts) 125 Pdr. RFA (4 Batt) 126 Pdr. RFA (3 Batt) 122 Bdr. RFA (2 Batts) Recommended necessary improvements all Amn. Inspected HqrS Coy & W. Trsm. Condition good.	
		2.0	Proceeded to CAUCOURT. Inspected No 3 Coy. D.A. COLUMN Condition good. Saw T. Major GAUCHIN-LEGAL re work required in village. Enquired re wire from field ambces required.	JBy
CAMBLAIN L'ABBE	4-8-16	8.30 HdQrs.	10 A.G. to Gov-Servins. Saw T. Major & NCO/c re fatigue work required & arranged to help with own party.	JBy

2449 Wt. W14957/Mg0 750,000 1/16 J.B.C. & A. Forms/C.2118/12.

Army Form C. 2118.

WAR DIARY or INTELLIGENCE SUMMARY

(Erase heading not required.)

SANITARY SECTION.
1ST LONDON (CITY OF LONDON) SANITARY CO

Instructions regarding War Diaries and Intelligence Summaries are contained in F. S. Regs., Part II. and the Staff Manual respectively. Title Pages will be prepared in manuscript.

Place	Date	Hour	Summary of Events and Information	Remarks and references to Appendices
CAMBLAIN L'ABBÉ	5-8-16	9-0 ASMS 9.45 10.15 2-0 2.0 9.15	ASMS 9.45 Staff Coyt. 103 Infy Bde called re supply of disinfectants to CAUCOURT. With MOYL Inspected area of DIV. AMM. COLUMN conditions very fair. Inspected Wagon Lines of 104 Bde RFA A & B Batty's & advised necessary improvements. Proceeded to GAUCHIN-LEGAL & advised re water supply re 125 Bde RFA camp. Saw T. Major re cleaning up in village re 125 Bde RFA. Reported re water supply to ADMS	
CAMBLAIN L'ABBÉ	6-8-16	9-0 ASMS 11-0 5.0	With DADMS Tour of inspection in village with DADMS Et ESTREE-CAUCHIE front near T. Major Re sanitation in village	
CAMBLAIN L'ABBÉ	7-8-16	8.30 ASMS 9-0 24, 25, 26, 27 2-0	With ADMS 9-0 to PETIT SERVINS. Inspected areas of NORTH & MIDDLESEX REGT. 103 Bde M. GUN COY TRANSPORT. Conditions fair. Recommended necessary improvements. With DADMS to BOIS DE BOUVIGNY. Saw MOYL 125 Bde RFA re sanitary matters. Proceeded to ABLAIN ST NAZAIRE. Conditions fair - owing to state of village.	
CAMBLAIN L'ABBÉ	8-8-16	8.30 ASMS 9-0 2-15 6.30	With ADMS to GAUCHIN-LEGAL. Made inspection of whole of area. Satisfactory. With ADMS to Trenches CARENCY Sector. Inspected various areas. Saw MOYL. Lea N/MIDDLESEX REGT & 104 YORKS & LANCS re sanitation #64 Infy. General report in village.	
CAMBLAIN L'ABBÉ	9-8-16			
CAMBLAIN L'ABBÉ	10-8-16	8.30 ASMS 9.45	To CARENCY with MOYLE Bde NORTH AND FUSILIERS inspected village. Conditions fair. Examined water supplies.	

2449 Wt. W14957/Mgo 750,000 1/16 J.B.C. & A. Forms/C.2118/12.

WAR DIARY or INTELLIGENCE SUMMARY

Army Form C. 2118.

SANITARY SECTION.
XXVII Division
1ST LONDON (CITY OF LONDON) SANITARY CO.

Place	Date	Hour	Summary of Events and Information	Remarks and references to Appendices
CAMBLAIN L'ABBE	11-8-16	8.30	ADMS Inspections in village	
		11.30	To BRUAY. Saw San. Off. of Div. Interchanged particulars of respective areas & arranged re discharging over of two San. Sections	
		4.30	Inspected area of DIV SUPPLY COLUMN. Advised improvements	HGY
CAMBLAIN L'ABBE	12-8-16	8.30	ADMS General duties in village. Arranged for re distribution of Section in new area	HGY
		5.0	Visited GROUP - SERVINS. Conditions in village greatly improved	HGY
		6.15	Saw NCO/c Squad re move	
CAMBLAIN L'ABBE	13-8-16	8.20	ADMS General duties in village	
		9.0	To ESTREE-CAUCHIE. Saw T. Major & NCO/c. Sting relieved	HGY
CAMBLAIN L'ABBE	14-8-16	8.15	ADMS. 8.30 Section proceeded to BRUAY	HGY
		11.30	Inspection made of area in town to be occupied	HGY
BRUAY	15-8-16	9.0	Tour of Billets, sanitary areas etc with NCO/c. Town made necessary arrangements. 10.30 Accompanied DADMS on inspection. Distributed Inspecting N.C.O.s over new Div. area.	HGY
BRUAY	16-8-16	8.30	ADMS. 9.45 To DIVISION Saw MO/c 24 NORTH-UMD FUSILIERS re sanitary arrangements. Visited BEUGIN & LA COMTE saw MOs of 4th MIDDLESEX & SOMERSETS re sanitation & carried out inspection of villages	
		3.0	Accompanied DADMS to GAUCHIN-LEGAL & CAUCOURT Inspected all water carts of R.F.A. & AMM. COLUMN	HGY
BRUAY	17-8-16	8.30	ADMS General duties. Inspections made in town	HGY
BRUAY	18-8-16	8.30	Army. 10.0 16 DIVISION Inspected Water carts of 24 NORTH-UMD FUSILIERS. Saw MO/c 24 NORTH-UMD FUSILIERS made inspections of village re sanitation	HGY
			Inspected Water Carts	
		2.30	To TRESNICOURT. Saw NCO/c village re sanitation & water supply	HGY

Army Form C. 2118.

WAR DIARY
or
INTELLIGENCE SUMMARY
(Erase heading not required.)

SANITARY SECTION,
XXVII DIVISION
1st LORDS AGH DIVISION NO. 39

Instructions regarding War Diaries and Intelligence Summaries are contained in F. S. Regs., Part II. and the Staff Manual respectively. Title Pages will be prepared in manuscript.

Place	Date	Hour	Summary of Events and Information	Remarks and references to Appendices
BRUAY	19.8.16	8.30 AM	Saw O/C HQ 1st F. Amb & advised re sanitation. Proceeded to OURTON & with MO/C inspected area of 37 NORTH'MD FUSILIERS. Both Progress made with sanitary arrangements.	
		3.0	Accompanied AA & QMG, DADMS, to HERNIN, FREVILLERS & La COMTE. Inspected sanitary areas & cookhouses. Progress very slow.	#GH
BRUAY	20.8.16	8.30 AM	General duties	
		5.0	To 63 Infy Bde HQrs. Inspected sanitary area & advised Staff Capt. on requirements for sanitation in Battalion areas.	#GH
			Visited N.C.O/c men	#GH
BRUAY	21.8.16	8.30 AM	to DIEVAL with MO/c & inspected areas of 8 LINES	#GH
		4.10	YORKS & LANCS. Progress good	
BRUAY	22.8.16	8.30 AM	Brigades changing over. Re-distributed dugouts.	
		2.0	to CAMBLAIN-CHATELAIN. Advised re Water Supply & am MO/c	#GH
		10	FUSILIERS re sanitary measures required.	
BRUAY	23.8.16	8.30 AM	General duties in town. Visited MO/c 112th Infy	
			Brigade, settled in town.	
		3.0	Lecture on "Sanitation in Cookhouses given to Cooking Class" #GH	
BRUAY	24.8.16	8.30 AM	10.0 to OURTON. Saw MO/C 13 RIFLE BDE re sanitation #GH	
BRUAY	25.8.16	8.30 AM	9.45 to DIVISION. with MO/c inspected area occupied by	
			13 KINGS ROYAL RFLS. Progress very slow	#GH
		2.30	Lecture "Sanitation in Cookhouses" to Cooking Class	#GH
BRUAY	26.8.16	8.30 AM	9.30 Accompanied AQMG on tour of inspection. Visited	
			Billets of DIV. ORDNANCE & DIV. SIGNALS. Satisfactory	#GH

Army Form C. 2118.

WAR DIARY
or
INTELLIGENCE SUMMARY
(Erase heading not required.)

SANITARY SECTION,
1ST LONDON CITY OF [illegible]

Place	Date	Hour	Summary of Events and Information	Remarks and references to Appendices
BRUAY	27.8.16	8.30 ADMS	General duties.	
BRUAY	28.8.16	8.30 ADMS. 9.50	BEGUIN. Proceeded to La Comté with M o/c 8 Black Watch. Went along inspected area. Advised necessary work still required.	
BRUAY	29.8.16	9.0 DADMS	General duties. Inspections in town.	
BRUAY	30.8.16	8.30 ADMS.	General duties. Inspections in town.	
BRUAY	31.8.16	8.30 ADMS.	General duties. 11-0 Inspected sanitary area & Billets Div. Signal Coy. 2-0 Inspected remainder of Billets Div. Signal Co.	

K Amos Capt
RAMC
O/C

Confidential. 140/1734/37

Sept. 1916

War Diary

of

Sanitary Section, 37th Division

from Sept 1st 1916 to Sept. 30th 1916

(Volume XIV)

M

H. Gray Capt
RAMC

o/c

COMMITTEE FOR THE
MEDICAL HISTORY OF THE WAR
Date 30 OCT 1916

WAR DIARY / INTELLIGENCE SUMMARY

Army Form C. 2118.

SANITARY SECTION,
XXVII Division
1ST LONDON (CITY OF LONDON) SANITARY CO.

Place	Date	Hour	Summary of Events and Information	Remarks and references to Appendices
BRUAY	1-9-16	8.30 ADMS 9-45 to BEUGIN, LA COMTE, FREVILLERS & HERMIN, saw NCO's in charge of these village re sundry matters waiting settlement. 2.30 Gate Lecture to Cooking Class.		
BRUAY	2-9-16	6.30 ADMS General duties & Inspections in town. 2.30 with ADMS inspected area of MOBILE VET. SECTION. Satisfactory. Also No 37 Supply Column, advised at improvements required to bathrooms & cook house (workshops)	
BRUAY	3-9-16	8.45 ADMS General duties. 6.0 ADMS Instructions re Class of Instruction to REGIMENTAL WATER DUTY MEN. Arranged program.	
BRUAY	4-9-16	8.30 ADMS 9.30 with ADMS to OURTON DIV. TRAIN. Satisfactory arrangements. Inspected areas of 6th BEDFS REGT & 5th EAST LANCS REGT. Proceeded to DIEVAL re improvement arrangements, slow, advised what required. 3.30 Visited DIV. GAS SCHOOL, LEFFREY TMR. Advised re any improvements in sanitary area.	
BRUAY	5-9-16	8.30 ADMS General duties & instructions in town.	
BRUAY	6-9-16	8.30 ADMS Class of instruction N.Co & WATER DUTY MEN commenced 8.45 to 9.30 Lecture Water Supplies 9.45-10.30 Lecture on Water Cart. Sterilization 10-45 to 12-0 Instruction on Water Cart. 2-0 to 4-0 Practical instruction WATER CART. 5-0 to Division visited NEDYC re sundry matters.	
BRUAY	7-9-16	8.30 ADMS 8.45 to 9.30 Instruction Lectures 10-0 to 12-0 Practical instruction WATER CART. 2-0 to 4-0 Practical instruction in cleaning & sterilizing tanks & fittings.	

WAR DIARY

INTELLIGENCE SUMMARY

(Erase heading not required.)

Army Form C. 2118.

SANITARY SECTION,
XXXVII Division
1ST LONDON CITY OF LONDON

Place	Date	Hour	Summary of Events and Information	Remarks and references to Appendices
BRUAY	8-9-16	8.30 ADMS 9.30 with ADMS to FREVILLERS, inspected area of 8 MIDDLESEX. Good progress made. Proceeded to HERMIN, inspected area of 8 SOMERSETS. Progress good, general conditions satisfactory. 2.30 Water Duty men Practical instruction on Water Cart. 8.45 to 12.0 } Instruction to W. Duty men by Section Staff Sergt. 2.0 to 4.0 }	163rd M. GUN COY HQrs Sergt HQrs
BRUAY	9-9-16	8.30 ADMS 9.30 to TRESNICOURT, inspected with MO i/c area of 8 LINCS REGT. Very satisfactory. Necessary work being carried out at cookhouses. 2.30 Examination of Water Duty Men generally intelligent. 8.45 ADMS 10.0 to DIVISION inspected sanitation at Refilling Point. Lids required for latrines, otherwise good. Proceeded to LA COMETTE inspected area of 152 Coy RE. Conditions good. 3.30 DADMS (San) 1st Army called. Divided latrines in Town.	HQrs HQrs
BRUAY	10-9-16	8.30 ADMS 9.30 with ADMS to BATUS, inspected area of 10th YORKS & LANCS REGT. Good progress made with sanitary management. Proceeded to DIEVAL and inspected area of 6 EAST LANCS REGT. Conditions good. Work still awaiting RE materials. Inspected 6 houses of 6th BEDFS REGT. Good. 2.0 with ADMS attended Conference of ADMS's & O/Co San. Sections at IV Corps DDMS.	HQrs HQrs
BRUAY	12-9-16	8.30 ADMS 9.30 to BEDGIN with MO i/c inspected area of 10 L. NORTH LANCS. Conditions good. Awaiting RE materials. Proceeded to LA COMTE approved sites for Cohouses & Ablution Benches. 2.30 to Coola Course of Instruction. 3.0 Examined W. Duty men attending Class of Instruction.	HQrs HQrs

Army Form C. 2118.

WAR DIARY
or
INTELLIGENCE SUMMARY
(Erase heading not required.)

SANITARY SECTION.
1ST LONDON CITY 38TH DIVISION.

Instructions regarding War Diaries and Intelligence Summaries are contained in F. S. Regs., Part II. and the Staff Manual respectively. Title Pages will be prepared in manuscript.

Place	Date	Hour	Summary of Events and Information	Remarks and references to Appendices
BRUAY	12-9-16	4.45	Inspection at Divl. GAS SCHOOL. Conditions now very good	#96
BRUAY	13-9-16	8.30 a.m.	Saw T. Major BRUAY re Sanitary arrangements to improve	
		10.0	To LA COMTE with NO/c Inspected area of 11 R. WARWICKS. Satisfactory	
		3.45	Visit of No 37 SUPPLY COL. re sanitary arrangements	#96
BRUAY	14-9-16	8.30 a.m.		
		10-0	To DIVISION saw M.O/c 9 NORTH STAFFS re Sanitary arrangements. Inspected two G. Houses, good conditions	#96
BRUAY	15-9-16	8.30 a.m.		
		9.45	Saw T. Major BRUAY, re improving Public Latrines	
		10-15	To BEUGIN. Saw MO/c re Officers Cookhouse unsatisfactorily just Myal at once	
			Proceeded to HOUDELIN saw NCO/c Village Sanitary matters. Proceeded to MAGNICOURT Inspected Spring.	#96
BRUAY	16-9-16	8.30 a.m.		
		9.40	To DIVISION with MO/c 4 2nd. 4/6. Inspected aux. Inhs & good progress being made	#96
BRUAY	17-9-16	8.40 a.m.	Advised re more 9.30 to BOYEFFLES, saw San. Officer re DIVN. conferred on work & arranged re changing over	#96
		2-15	Received movement orders	
BRUAY	18-9-16	8.20 a.m.	General clearing up. 11.30 San. Officer 23rd. DIVN called. Handed over. Received & Inferred him over Billets, Store Room etc	#96
BRUAY	19-9-16	8.30	Section moved to BOYEFFLES. 8.50 Visited H.Q.H.S.	#96
BOYEFFLES	19-9-16	10.0	Self arrived BOYEFFLES, arranged Billets etc	
		2.0	To BARLIN with DADMS & NCO/c made tour re Water Supply & sanitary arrangements	#96
BOYEFFLES	20-9-16	8.30	General tour re sanitation	
		12.0	with San. Officer 9th & 4th DIVN. Proceeded to LILLERS to Hold a Conference of San. Officers with DMS 1st. Army. Views expressed & exchanged	#96

Army Form C. 2118.

SANITARY SECTION.
XXVII Division
1ST LONDON (CITY OF LONDON BATTALION)

WAR DIARY
or
INTELLIGENCE SUMMARY
(Erase heading not required.)

Place	Date	Hour	Summary of Events and Information	Remarks and references to Appendices
BOYEFFLES	21-9-16	8:30	General duties & inspections in village	
		2-0	to HERSIN-COUPIGNY. Made general inspection. Unoccupied Billets in filthy condition. Reported to TOWN MAJOR. Company huts very bad. Sanitation reported.	HL/4
BOYEFFLES	22-9-16	9:45	to BULLY GRENAY. General condition very dusty, being cleaned up along	
		3:45	to BARLIN, visited ADMS	
BOYEFFLES	23-9-16	6:30	Orderly Room. 11:45 to BRUAY met San. Officers 9th, 24th & 2nd Divns. Proceeded to LA GORGUE inspected workshops of West Lan Section. Latrines & Furniture models rather elaborate.	HL/4
		4:0	Visited ADMD.	
BOYEFFLES	24-9-16		General duties. 7-0 ADMS called. 7:30 O/C 49th F. Amb called. HCL/4.	
BOYEFFLES	25-9-16	8:30	O. Room. 9:45 to BULLY-GRENAY. Proceeded to CALONNE. Good water supply good sanitary arrangements. Great deal of rubbish about	HL/4
		3:15	NSMD.	
BOYEFFLES	26-9-16	8:20	O. Room. 9:45 to BARLIN with DADMS & N Cork inspected Sanitation of Hy Chld. (Progressing) improvements still required.	
		5:0	Visited Div Signals, Laun, advised improvements req with re Sanitation.	
BOYEFFLES	27-9-16	8:30	O. Room. 10:0 to FOSSE 10. With MO/C inspected Hq & 2 Coys of NORTH STAFFS REGT. Condition good.	
		3:0	to BOIS de BOUVIGNY. General conditions bad. Reported to ADMS (verbally)	HL/4

Army Form C. 2118.

SANITARY SECTION,
XXVII [?]
1st LONDON (CITY OF LONDON) SANITARY Co.

WAR DIARY
or
INTELLIGENCE SUMMARY
(Erase heading not required.)

Instructions regarding War Diaries and Intelligence Summaries are contained in F.S. Regs., Part II. and the Staff Manual respectively. Title Pages will be prepared in manuscript.

Place	Date	Hour	Summary of Events and Information	Remarks and references to Appendices
BOYEFFLES	28.9.16		8:30 O.Room 10.0 to HERSIN. General tour of inspection. Work in hand but progress slow. Inspected Wagon Lines 123 Bde "B", very fair. Transport 11 ROYL WARWICKS, fair. 3.30 to BARLIN saw ADMS & DADMS & reported progress.	AGh
BOYEFFLES	29.9.16		8:30 O.Room 9:45 to BULLY with MO/c. Inspected area of 13 ROY. FUSILIERS, very fair. Also area occupied 111th Bde Hqrs. Extensive cleaning up work required.	AGh
BOYEFFLES	30.9.16		8:45 O.Room 9:45 to BARLIN with DADMS & NCO/c inspected area of DAC "A" & "B". Very fair.	AGh

H Gross Capt
RAMC
O/c

[Stamp: SANITARY SECTION No. 307 Date 1/9/16 37th DIVISION]

Confidential.

War Diary
of

37th Sanitary Section, 37th Division

from Oct 1st 1916 to Oct 31st 1916.

(Volume XV)

To:-
A.D.M.S.
37th Division

SANITARY SECTION
No. 10
Date 31/16
37th DIVISION

War Diary

Herewith War Diary for the month of October 1916.

H.S.Moss
Capt. R.A.M.C.
O/C Sanitary Section
37th Division

Army Form C. 2118.

WAR DIARY
INTELLIGENCE SUMMARY
(Erase heading not required.)

SANITARY SECTION.
XXXVII Division
1ST LONDON CO[...] Sanitary S[ection]

Place	Date	Hour	Summary of Events and Information	Remarks and references to Appendices
BOYEFFLES	1-10-16		General duties.	
BOYEFFLES	2-10-16	9.45	To AIX-NOULETTE. Made inspection of 124 Bde Batteries with M.O. Very satisfactory progress. Advised M.O. re water supply for drinking. Called at H.Qrs. 124 Bde re cleaning up of village & arranged for fatigue parties. Workshops in full working order.	#54/1 #54/2
BOYEFFLES	3-10-16	9.45	To BARLIN with D.A.D.M.S. inspected Sanitary arrangements at DIV. HQRS. and DIV. TRAIN. Very satisfactory.	
		3.30	Visited CRE. re tools for Workshops & supply of materials &c.	
BOYEFFLES	4-10-16	10.0	To AIX-NOULETTE and BOIS DE NOULETTE with M.O. Inspected encampment of 10 YORKS & LANCS REGT. Conditions good. Inspected Wells at AIX-NOULETTE & requisted ones for use.	#55/1 #55/2
BOYEFFLES	5-10-16	9.30	To BULLY-GRENAY. Called 11 Bde Hqrs. re fatigue party for CALONNE. Proceeded to CALONNE. Made inspection. Conditions greatly improved.	
		3.0	To HERSIN. Saw Transport-Officer, 13 Kings Royal Rifles, re sanitation of camp.	
BOYEFFLES	6-10-16	10.0	To BULLY. N.C.O. i/c made inspection of BOYEFFLES. Generally satisfactory. Gone dwelt 13 R. Bde TRANS condemned, men removed at once.	
		2.15	Proceeded to BOIS DE BOUVIGNY & made thorough inspection. No work going on. A great deal of cleaning up required &c.	
		9.30	To BARLIN. Reported to DADMS.	
BOYEFFLES	7-10-16		N.C.O. i/c inspected area of 13 R. FUSILIERS & 13 K ROYAL RFLS. Transport & i/c to Col Shelton. Proceeded to HERSIN, & with A BATTY. 124 Bde WAGON LINES. Few advised improvements required. Also inspected 124 Bde improvements.	#54/4

*Army Form C. 2118.

WAR DIARY
INTELLIGENCE SUMMARY
(Erase heading not required.)

SANITARY SECTION.
1ST LONDON (XXXVII) Division.

Instructions regarding War Diaries and Intelligence Summaries are contained in F.S. Regs., Part II. and the Staff Manual respectively. Title Pages will be prepared in manuscript.

Place	Date	Hour	Summary of Events and Information	Remarks and references to Appendices
BOYEFFLES	8/10/16		General duties.	HQly
BOYEFFLES	9/10/16		General duties.	HQly
BOYEFFLES	10/10/16	9.30	to BARLIN. Reported DADMS. Proceeded to HERSIN & mt NCO &/c inspected Transport Lines 11 ROYAL WARWICKS & 10 R. FUSILIERS. Condition good. Also Wagons Lines 124 Bde "C". Good. And 123 Bde "D". Advised many improvements required.	
BOYEFFLES	11/10/16	2.15	to BOIS DE BOUVIGNY made inspection, little work done of shelters.	HQly
		9.45	to FOSSE 10 Arranged G.H. Inspections for Battalion & reoccupy small units with Cpl C. Also inspected area of 13B R.G.A.	
		4	Saw O/C re conforming to Divisional sanitary requirements	
		4.30	to BARLIN reported to ADMS & DADMS.	
BOYEFFLES	12/10/16	10.0	to FOSSE 10 Approved G.H. sites for 2 Batts & shelters already being erected.	HQly
			Proceeded to AIX-NOULETTE, inspected & registered all wells in village. Called on 63 Bde HQrs re work required at BOIS DE BOUVIGNY & got matter put in hand.	
		2.0	Attended Gas Course at Div. GAS SCHOOL.	
BOYEFFLES	13/10/16	9.45	to BARLIN reported to ADMS. Advised re more Fly Units for Water Carts. Saw DADOS re Stores required. Saw NCO i/c BARLIN re sundry matters.	HQly
BOYEFFLES	14/10/16	10.30	to BARLIN Reported DADMS. Saw NCO i/c BARLIN. Made arrangements re mort.	HQly

Army Form C. 2118.

WAR DIARY
INTELLIGENCE SUMMARY
(Erase heading not required.)

SANITARY SECTION,
XXXVII 2ND DIST
1ST LONDON CITY OF LONDON SANITARY GP.

Instructions regarding War Diaries and Intelligence Summaries are contained in F. S. Regs., Part II. and the Staff Manual respectively. Title Pages will be prepared in manuscript.

Place	Date	Hour	Summary of Events and Information	Remarks and references to Appendices
BOYEFFLES	15.10.16		General duties with Section. 11.0 Reported to ADMS. Received instructions re move. Arranged to attach Squad to each HAmber to supervise sanitation of Bivy on march.	#94
BOYEFFLES	16.10.16		General duties with Section. 11.30 Reported to ADMS. 12.0 Proceeded to ROELLECOURT. Made Sanitary survey, also investigated water supply. 5.15 Reported to ADMS. Result of visit.	#94
BOYEFFLES	17.10.16		Inspected Section equipment etc & made arrangements re move. 5.0 Reported to ADMS. Received instructions re move.	#94
BOYEFFLES	18.10.16		Left BOYEFFLES at 8.45 for ROELLECOURT, via FRESNICOURT, HERMIN, CHELERS. Arrived ROELLECOURT 3-50. 20 mile march. Arranged Billets etc.	#94
ROELLECOURT	19.10.16		Rested. Inspected Sanitation at Div. Hqrs.	#94
ROELLECOURT	20.10.16	9.15	Left for LE CAUROY. Arrived 12.30. Arranged Billets etc. Arranged Sanitation at DIV. HQRS.	#94
LE CAUROY	21.10.16	9.15	Left for BEAUVAL via FICHEUX, DOULLENS. Arrived 3.30. Arranged Billets etc and Sanitation DIV. HQRS.	#94
BEAUVAL	22.10.16	9.15	Left for MARIEUX, arrived 11.45. Arranged Billets etc & Sanitation & water supply Div. HQRS.	#94
MARIEUX	23.10.16	9.0	ADMS. No orders. Arranged duties for Section. 2.30 made inspection of half village with T.M.ajor re evacuation of Battalion. Satisfactory. 4.0 ADMS. No orders to move. Foden Disinfector attached to Section.	#94

2449 Wt. W14957/M90 750,000 1/16 J.B.C. & A. Forms/C.2118/12.

Army Form C. 2118.

WAR DIARY
or
INTELLIGENCE SUMMARY

(Erase heading not required.)

SANITARY SECTION.
1ST ... XXXVII DIVISION 2ND SANITARY CO.

Instructions regarding War Diaries and Intelligence Summaries are contained in F. S. Regs., Part II. and the Staff Manual respectively. Title Pages will be prepared in manuscript.

Place	Date	Hour	Summary of Events and Information	Remarks and references to Appendices
MARIEUX	24-10-16	9.0	ADMS. No orders. Re-arranged distribution of Section. Arranged for N.C.Os to inspect districts from H.qrs. Arranged Baths for DN. H.QRS. Units.	H.G.F.
MARIEUX	25-10-16	9.0	ADMS. Duties with Section. I/o Received instructions to investigate water supply at PUCH ANDRE.	
		3.0	Proceeded to ARQUEVES, picked up RE Officer & proceeded to HAMEL. Took samples from water at MILL & at BRIDGE near MIRAUMONT.	
MARIEUX	26-10-16	9.0	ADMS. Made analysis on water samples. Satisfactory.	H.G.F.
MARIEUX	27-10-16	9.30	ADMS. Assisted M.O/c 8 EAST LANCS re arranging Baths. General duties with Section. Disinfected 560 Blankets for 8 E. LANCS.	H.G.F.
MARIEUX	28-10-16	9.30	ADMS. 10.30 to PUCHEVILLERS. Made sanitary survey with M.O/c 13 K.R. Rifles and 13 R. Fusiliers. Satisfactory.	H.G.F.
		2.30	Inspected Water Supply, sterilizing apparatus at THIEVRES. General duties with Section.	H.G.F.
MARIEUX	29-10-16		General duties with Section, workshop etc.	H.G.F.
MARIEUX	30-10-16	9.30	Reported to ADMS. 10.30 to SARTON. Inspected Cookers of 6 BEDS. REGT. fairly satisfactory, also inspected Water Carts, in excellent condition. Proceeded to ORVILLE saw 37 DIV. AMM. COLUMN, just taking up position.	H.G.F.
MARIEUX	31-10-16		Very unsatisfactory. Reported to ADMS.	H.G.F.

H. Smog Capt
o/c Sanitary Section
37 Division

SANITARY SECTION
Date 31/10/16
37th DIVISION

140/1862
Vol 16

Confidential

War Diary

of

Sanitary Section, 37th Division

from Nov 1st 1916 to Nov. 30th 1916.

(Volume XVI)

COMMITTEE FOR THE
MEDICAL HISTORY OF THE WAR
Date -3 JAN. 1917

H Grice Capt
RAMC
O/C

SANITARY SECTION
37th DIVISION

Army Form C. 2118.

WAR DIARY
of
INTELLIGENCE SUMMARY.
(Erase heading not required.)

SANITARY SECTION,
XXXVII DIVISION
1ST LONDON (CITY OF LONDON) SANITARY CO.

Instructions regarding War Diaries and Intelligence Summaries are contained in F.S. Regs., Part II. and the Staff Manual respectively. Title pages will be prepared in manuscript.

Place	Date	Hour	Summary of Events and Information	Remarks and references to Appendices
MARIEUX	1-11-16	9.30 A&MS	Inspected W/Carts 13 R.FUSILIERS & 13 KINGS ROYAL RIFLES. Satisfactory.	
		2.30	MESNIL Inspected Water Supply at Dump and advised re Earth & Petrol Tins.	
MARIEUX	2-11-16	7.0	Reported to A&MS + 'Q' Office re work done.	
		9.30 A&MS	Received instructions from DADMS re Water Dump, MESNIL & sent out party to supplement troops.	
			General duties with Section.	
MARIEUX	3-11-16	9.30 A&MS	Saw DADMS re party for MESNIL & sent party off.	
		10.30 to BEAVAL	With MO/c 9 N. STAFFS REGT inspected Water Carts, Billets & Unit. Conditions fair.	
			Saw MO/c H/d MIDDLESEX REGT re Sanitation of Unit & Water Carts.	
		6.0 A&MS	Reported re condition of Public Latrines at BEAUVAL & GEZAIN-COURT.	
MARIEUX	4-11-16	9.0	Reported to DADMS re work done at MESNIL. Reported to ADMS.	
		10.30 to HEM.	Saw MO/c 1 D.R.FUSILIERS re Water Carts & Sanitation.	
			Proceeded to LONGUEVILLETTE. Inspected Sanitation of village. Satisfactory.	
MARIEUX	5-11-16	9.15 A&MS	General duties with Section.	
			Inspected Sanitation of Hqrs. Unit. Satisfactory.	
MARIEUX	6-11-16	9.15 A&MS	10-15 to TERRA MESNIL. With MO/c inspected Billets, Cookhouse, Water Carts etc of 10 YORKS & LANCS REGT. Satisfactory. Arranged re disinfection of Blankets.	
MARIEUX	7-11-16	9.30 W/A&MS	General duties with Section	
MARIEUX	8-11-16	9-15 A&MS	General duties with Section	

WAR DIARY
INTELLIGENCE SUMMARY
(Erase heading not required.)

Army Form C. 2118

SANITARY SECTION.
XXXVII Division
1ST LONDON SANITARY CO

Place	Date	Hour	Summary of Events and Information	Remarks and references to Appendices
MARIEUX	9-11-16		9-10 ADMS 10-0 to DOULLENS with MO/c & EAST LANCS inspected Water Carts, Cookhouses, Billets etc. Satisfactory.	HQy
MARIEUX	10-11-16		9-10 ADMS 10-0 to BEAUVAL with MO/c 6 SOMERSETS REGT inspected sanitation of area, Water Carts etc – Conditions fair. 2-15 ADMS re Operations 3-0 Lecture to Section Sanitation & Water. Duties in area 5-0 ADMS re Operations	HQy HQy HQy
MARIEUX	11-11-16		9-0 ADMS. 10-0 to SARTON with MO/c 6th BEDS REGT inspected Billets, Cookhouses, Sanitary areas of Unit. Conditions very satisfactory.	HQy
MARIEUX	12-11-16		9-0 ADMS. Duties with Section	HQy
MARIEUX	13-11-16		Duties with Section.	HQy
MARIEUX	14-11-16		9-45 Proceeded to VARENNES reported to DADMS for instructions	HQy
MARIEUX	15-11-16		Waiting orders. Duties with Section	HQy
MARIEUX	16-11-16	10-15	Orders received from ADMS to proceed to HEDAUVILLE. Section left. 10-45 and arrived at HEDAUVILLE 3-15.	HQy
HEDAUVILLE	17-11-16	10-30	Section proceeded to FORCEVILLE. Settled in arranged Billets. Stores, Sanitary accommodation etc.	HQy
FORCEVILLE	18-11-16		Section on duty in village	HQy
FORCEVILLE	19-11-16		Capt MOSS evacuated sick to No 2 General Hospital. B.A.B.M.S. took over duties of Sanitary Section officer	HQy
FORCEVILLE	20-11-16		Section on duty in village	C.b Tucherne
FORCEVILLE	21-11-16		Section on duty in village	C.b Tucherne

Army Form C. 2118.

WAR DIARY
or
INTELLIGENCE SUMMARY.
(Erase heading not required.)

Instructions regarding War Diaries and Intelligence Summaries are contained in F. S. Regs., Part II. and the Staff Manual respectively. Title pages will be prepared in manuscript.

SANITARY SECTION.
1ST LONDON (OR 56TH LONDON) SANITARY Cº

Place	Date	Hour	Summary of Events and Information	Remarks and references to Appendices
FORCEVILLE	22.11.16		Two N.C.O's sent to ENGLEBELMER for inspection of billets occupied by 111th Brigade. Conditions unsatisfactory owing to many different troops passing through.	C.6. Tarbun
FORCEVILLE	23.11.16		Two N.C.O's to ENGLEBELMER and inspected area & battalion water carts. N.C.O's to ENGLEBELMER tested & effected fit for cooking. 2 wells in ENGLEBELMER unfit for division train & billets unfit. N.C.O's to LEALVILLERS to inspect billets of division train & billets unfit. Area in satisfactory condition.	C.6. Tarbun C.6. Tarbun
FORCEVILLE	24.11.16		Sanitary improvements in ENGLEBELMER now occupied by 63rd Brigade. Section Lorry driver to MARIEUX this day.	C.6. Tarbun
FORCEVILLE	25.11.16		Section proceeded to MARIEUX. Section marched starting at 9 a.m. Arrival MARIEUX at 2 p.m.	C.6. Tarbun
MARIEUX	26.11.16		111th Brigade at PUCHEVILLERS. Party sent to inspect area. About also sent to TERRAMESNIL & SARTON in advance of arrival in towns. Conditions in PUCHEVILLERS unsatisfactory. Areas left in filthy condition. C.6. Tarbun	C.6. Tarbun
MARIEUX	27.11.16		Same parties visited PUCHEVILLERS, SARTON, TERRAMESNIL. Reports from medical officers of the battalions of the 111th Brigade collected the 10th & 13th Royal Fusiliers in huts which are not at PUCHEVILLERS. Own accommodation and general sanitary arrangements unsatisfactory. The 13th K.R.R.C. in billets reported by weather front Somme sad.	
MARIEUX	28.11.16		The Medical officer of the battalion very unsatisfactory.	

A.5834 Wt. W4973/M687 750,000 8/16 D. D. & L. Ltd. Forms/C.2118/13

WAR DIARY of INTELLIGENCE SUMMARY.

Army Form C. 2118.

(Erase heading not required.)

SANITARY SECTION,
1ST LONDON (CITY OF LONDON) SAN. UN. CO.

Place	Date	Hour	Summary of Events and Information	Remarks and references to Appendices
MARIEUX	29-11-16		D.A.D.M.S. visited billets of 13th K.R.R.C. Many barns have the ground covered with thirdelen in wet manure with implement odour. The men have to lie on the ground. The farm yards are all in a very unsatisfactory condition – no drainage – most of the ground available is FOUL GROUND. In some places there are big piles of unburnt refuse. Incinerators in insufficient quantity. Every available effort is being made to improve conditions. The worst billets are being fumigated with O.G.T. and disinfectants.	
MARIEUX	30-11-16		Visited huts of 10th & 13th K.R.7's PUCHEVILLERS. There have been no arrangements for proper drains. The battalions have dug trenches around the huts & the mud churned up. As much sand as possible is being carted in many huts the ground is still very damp. There is no drainage. In a large abbution trench of the 13th K.R.7's, & the water is running into the ground around & into the mud. The huts have been no cover. The cookhouses & a running adequate. Beds have been dug to drain. Many improvements are still necessary. The stench dug to drain. Many improvements are still necessary. O.G.T. mud is being cleared from all around the cookhouses & a As soon as there is rain the conditions will rapidly become worse.	

P.C. Treherne
Captain R.A.M.C.
Commanding Sanitary Section,
37th Division.

Dec 1916   40/905   Vol 17

Confidential

War Diary

of

Sanitary Section, 37th Division.

From Dec 1st 1916 to Dec 31st 1916.

(Volume XVII)

COMMITTEE FOR THE
MEDICAL HISTORY OF THE WAR
Date 31 JAN. 1917

A W Beasley Lieut. RAMC
O/C

[Stamp: SANITARY SECTION 37th DIVISION]

Army Form C. 2118.

WAR DIARY
or
INTELLIGENCE SUMMARY.
(Erase heading not required.)

Instructions regarding War Diaries and Intelligence Summaries are contained in F.S. Regs., Part II. and the Staff Manual respectively. Title pages will be prepared in manuscript.

SANITARY SECTION

Place	Date	Hour	Summary of Events and Information	Remarks and references to Appendices
MARIEUX	1.12.16		9th N. Staffords marched from MAILLY to RAINCHEVAL. RAINCHEVAL was evacuated by the 63rd Bde H.Q. - 63rd Bn. E. Coy. - 63rd T.M. Battery - 8 tenements & 10 DS lorries yesterday 30.11.16, & the village was left in a satisfactory condition. B.A.D.M.S. supper.	D.G.T.
MARIEUX	2.12.16		Handed over Sanitary Return to Lieut: S. CHILD R.A.M.C. General conditions in PUCHEVILLERS improving. Fresh latrines & urine pits being dug. Incinerators not minimum enough.	D.G.T.
MARIEUX	3.12.16		Several duties with Section. 8km to BEAUQUESNE and started to School of Sanitation.	S.C.
MARIEUX	4.12.16		General duties. Preparations for Army School Sanitation in MARIEUX.	
MARIEUX	5.12.16		General duties with Section.	
MARIEUX	6.12.16		Visit to SARTON on receipt of complaints from D.O.S. Whartin Rattray rectifying condition of latrines. Condition found unsatisfactory referred to M.D.M.S.	
MARIEUX	7.12.16		Inauguration of Sanitary Divisional School at MARIEUX. Visit No 43 Billet MARIEUX on complaint of Town Major.	
MARIEUX	8.12.16		9 a.m. School Sanitation - 12. 2.30 School 3. Visit Public Latrine & Town Major MARIEUX inadequate additional accommodation required. What's P.A.D.M.S. G.S.O.t. - MIRLEUX C.R.E. Park arrived condition unsatisfactory class started.	
MARIEUX	9.12.16		9.15. Parade School Sanitation - MIRLEUX interview with officer in detailed fatigue party to remedy. Latrines tents overflowing no ground.	

Army Form C. 2118.

WAR DIARY
or
INTELLIGENCE SUMMARY.
(Erase heading not required.)

SANITARY SECTION.

19 10 ... ... JANUARY 19

Instructions regarding War Diaries and Intelligence Summaries are contained in F. S. Regs., Part II. and the Staff Manual respectively. Title pages will be prepared in manuscript.

Place	Date	Hour	Summary of Events and Information	Remarks and references to Appendices
MARIEUX	10.12.18	-	School of Sanitation. Several duties with Section	
MARIEUX	11.12.18		School of Sanitation. Visited Gerton SARTON inspecting Native accommodation. M.O. & Lieuts. and J. Myer out. arrangement made for full lecture at H.Q. Millet & lucern in front of deaf hut which owing of land agent to	
MARIEUX	12.12.18		School of Sanitation. 1st Class dismissed. 2nd Class cancelled owing to orders received of movement of Divisions.	
MARIEUX	13.12.18		Several duties with Section	
FROHEN LE GRAND	14.12.18		Division moved. No Section arrived FROHEN LE GRAND.	
FLERS	15-17.12.18		Section left FROHEN LE GRAND 9am arrived at FLERS	
Monchy Cayan	16.12.18		Section left FLERS arrived at MONCHY CAYAN.	
NORRENTES - FONTES	17.12.18	9	Section left MONCHY CAYAN arrived at NORRENTES FONTES 4pm.	
ST VENANT	18.12.18	9	Section left NORRENTES FONTES arrived at ST VENANT	
ST VENANT	19.12.18		General duties with Section	
ST VENANT	20.12.18		" " S.O. LESTREM out S.O. St Dw.	
LESTREM	21.12.18		Section left ST VENANT for LESTREM.	
LESTREM	22.12.18		LIEUT BESCOBY arrived & took over duty as S.O.	

Army Form C. 2118.

WAR DIARY
or
INTELLIGENCE SUMMARY.
(Erase heading not required.)

SANITARY SECTION.
1ST LONDON (47TH OF 56TH DIV.) SANITARY CO.

Place	Date	Hour	Summary of Events and Information	Remarks and references to Appendices
LESTREM	23/12/16		Took over Section from Lieut. Child. R.A.M.C. Went to La Gorge to determine boundaries of area of 56th Div. Organisation of work for area.	acB
"	24/12/16		Arranging billets &c. with Camp Commandant. To Merville to O.C. 3rd Mobile Laboratory.	acB
"	25/12/16		Headquarters. Gen. Sanitation, recommendations concerning. Arrangement of fatigue party obtained by Town Major. Commenced local necessary structures - latrine, ablution benches. Obtained first billet for men.	acB
"	26/12/16		District of Section now area of general organisation. To VIEILLE CHAPELLE & BOUT DEVILLE.	acB
"	27/12/16		Further work at Hqrs. Office. Case suspected Cerebro Spinal - Meningitis reported - Action taken.	acB
"	28/12/16		Disinfection of billet & suspects (S.M.) To Trenches with D.A.D.M.S. Visited Div. Transport with O.C.	acB
"	29/12/16		Arranged further details with A.D.M.S., Camp Commandant. To LES HUIT MAISONS. Visited 111th M.G. Coys. with O.C. 2/13th R.F. with O.C. (CROIX BARBÉE) Recommendations made.	acB
"	30/12/16		To VIEILLE CHAPELLE & LA COUTURE with Town Major, to investigate case of Diphtheria in civil population. To LOCON to see civil doctor. Exam. of bath &c. with D.A.D.M.S.	acB
"	31/12/16		To CROIX BARBÉE to visit 10th R.F. Inspection of section & attached men.	acB

A.C.Beecroft LtRAMC.
San. Off. 37th Div.

37 Vol 18

40/943

Confidential
War Diary
—of—
Sanitary Section, 37th Division

from January 1st 1917 to January 31st 1917

Volume XVIII

COMMITTEE FOR THE
MEDICAL HISTORY OF THE WAR
Date 13 MAR. 1917

Lieut. RAMC
Albuerty
O/c Sanitary Section
37th Division

Army Form C. 2118.

WAR DIARY
or
INTELLIGENCE SUMMARY.
(Erase heading not required.)

No. 37 SANITARY SECTION

1915

Instructions regarding War Diaries and Intelligence Summaries are contained in F.S. Regs. Part II. and the Staff Manual respectively. Title pages will be prepared in manuscript.

Place	Date	Hour	Summary of Events and Information	Remarks and references to Appendices
LESTREM	Jan. 1.		Inspected billets 9 areas, CROIX BARBÉE and VIEILLE CHAPELLE. To Town Major re fatigue party. Visited case diphtheria in civil population & arranged for disinfection, isolation & contacts in conjunction with civil doctor.	A03
do.	Jan. 2		To PARADIS to M.O.R.S. Generals. To HINGES (Field Cashier). Visited Sanitary Stn at LOCON. To C.R.E. duPAUX. Inspected 5. E. Lancs. 9 visited C.O. & M.O. To LOCON to superintend removal of slops	A03
do.	Jan. 3		To CALONNE-SUR-LYS for DISINFECTION OF BILLETS. To Town Major re sanitation of VIEILLE CHAPELLE. Visited Esteminets & Canteens. Visited fatigue parties working from H.Qs.	A03
do.	Jan. 4		Inspected A.S.C. at FOSSE with Adjutant. Changed men's billets to better quarters. Constructional work at H.Q. Gap refreshing maunaus	A03
do.	Jan. 5		Paid men in out-lying districts. Inspected 13 R.F. transport. Reported midden at R.29.C.1.1.6 to Town Major, VIEILLE CHAPELLE & arranged for improvement. Visited pumping station & reported to A.D.M.S. & C.R.E. Visited civil case diphtheria at Le Touret with M.O. Bedfords, & arranged with A.D.M. to place house (billet & treatment) out of bounds. Constructional work at H.Q. (proceeds)	
do.	Jan. 6		To PARADIS to take sample water. To O.C. No. 3 Mobile Lab., MERVILLE. Paid men & section. To Ordnance. To LOCON. Inspected Gas School & Town Sanitation Generally. Fitted Box respirators & inspected P.H. helmets. Interviewed D.A.D.O.S. re latrine buckets owing to nature of country, which makes digging impossible.	A03
do.	Jan. 7.		Church parade. To FOSSE to 8th Lincolns M.O. Inspected men's meals & billets. To ESTAIRES.	
do.	Jan. 8.		Inspected billets of 9th North Staff. To PARADIS re water supply. Arranged San. details Y.M.C.A. huts.	A03
do.	Jan. 9.		Inspected billets of 126 Bde R.F.A. with M.O. Arranged for more effective removal of manure. To PARADIS, PACAUT & QUENTIN (portions of D.A.C.)	

Army Form C. 2118.

WAR DIARY
or
INTELLIGENCE SUMMARY.
(Erase heading not required.)

No. 37 SANITARY SECTION.
1st [?] SANITARY Co

Instructions regarding War Diaries and Intelligence Summaries are contained in F.S. Regs., Part II. and the Staff Manual respectively. Title pages will be prepared in manuscript.

Place	Date	Hour	Summary of Events and Information	Remarks and references to Appendices
LESTREM	Jan 10		Visited A Batt'y Lines, 124 Bde R.F.A. with O.C. Saw Town Major VIEILLE CHAPELLE re Horsfall incinerator &c. Visited 111th M.G.C. Received numerous requests re lime for field washing kitchens & billets.	acs
do	Jan 11		To LOCON to take men's material for disinfection of billets. Impeded water station LACOUTURE & reports of men re CRE & ADMS. To MERVILLE for medical stores. Saw Camp Commandant re provision of material for use of section working at Hqrs.	aes
do	Jan 12		Saw ADMS, CRE, D"Q" re provision of Horsfall incinerator for area. With Camp Commandant to PARADIS to arrange for portion of field for erection of larger workshop. Work commenced on this.	acs
do	Jan 13		To LOCON for material in use of G-box incinerator. To LE TOURET and VIEILLE CHAPELLE re material for Town Sanitation. Visited Town Major. To Staff Captain 112 Bde re sanitation & listing of box incineration attached Bde's men. To M.O. 11th Warwicks, re case of measles collected P.H.G. helmets. Impeded area A & B 6/9 L.N. Lancs. Ardleuin well VIEILLE CHAPELLE. Source examined.	acs
do	Jan 14		To Guichen (NEUVE CHAPELLE) with D.A.D.M.S. Reported on Water Supply. Source examined. Impeded billets Regt headquarters.	acs
do	Jan 15		To A.D.S. LE TOURET, re case of Diphtheria. Saw Lt Mence & Cap't Evans (124 Bde R.F.A.) re a recent case in area. To A.P.M. re isolation of detainments. Interviewed adjt R.E. about material from R.A.M.C. civil population. To A.P.M. re reports of temporary laundry (building protector(?)). From 48th F.A. reports for maintain. To MERVILLE men with M.O. & pellets pills for maintain. Visited area with pump opinion. To Ordnance re material for section & provision of latrine buckets for area.	acs
do	Jan 16		To Les Lorbe's & St Venants Mobile Lab with sample opinion. To O.C. No. 3. Saw S.S.O. re supply of bleaching powder, & CRE for material for incinerators. Obtained behind lime for water supply for trenches. Six machines reported for duty.	ac9
do	Jan 17		Sent car to LE TOURET to take water (offered to test supplies Seg't of section detailed to supervise building of incineration & materials transports. Moved attached men to permanent billet - TO HINGES (feels Cashin) & BETHUNE (Clayton disinfector)	acs

Army Form C. 2118.

WAR DIARY
or
INTELLIGENCE SUMMARY.
(Erase heading not required.)

SANITARY SECTION,
1st SOUTH MIDLAND SANITARY Cº

Instructions regarding War Diaries and Intelligence Summaries are contained in F. S. Regs., Part II. and the Staff Manual respectively. Title pages will be prepared in manuscript.

Place	Date	Hour	Summary of Events and Information	Remarks and references to Appendices
LESTREM	Jan. 18		To LES LOBES (Incinerator). To La C¹⁴ MARMEUSE (8ᵗʰ Somersets). No 10 Kᵗᵉ Balloon Section. Received report re samples of bleaching powder. Both much under strength.	acs
	Jan. 19		To LES 8 MAISONS, VIEILLE CHAPELLE & LE TOURET. To LES LOBES, ? R.E. yard. To CRE, ? A.A. ? M.G. Pass section at Hqrs attached to M.O. 8ᵗʰ Somersets. To	acs
	Jan. 20		Collected material for sanitary purposes. Superintended construction work at Hqrs. Interviewed C.O. Signal Co & Camp Commandant re Sanitary Matters.	acs
	Jan. 21		To LOCON to meet O.C. 152 Cᵒʸ R.E. to fix site of Hospital destructor with D.A.D.M.S. To R.E. dump LE TOURET, re proposed pas de diphtheria. To PARADIS to interview M.O. ⅟₁ D.A.C.	acs
	Jan. 22		To 48ᵗʰ F.A. with casualty. To 50ᵗʰ F.A. ? adjt ? N. Staff re accumulation of rubbish. To 111ᵗʰ M.G.Cʸ re adverse report on water cart. To LES LOBES & LA Cⁱᵉ MARMEUSE to see completed incinerator. Inspected 13ᵗʰ KRR transport at BOUT DEVILLE & 13ᵗʰ R.F. at (CROIX BARBÉE)	acs
	Jan. 23		To 49ᵗʰ F.A. To R.E. dump, LE TOURET. To trenches (F---- du BOIS sector) no water supply. To LOCON re cases of diphtheria.	acs
	Jan. 24		Met R.E. officer at LOCON to select site for destructor. Rendered monthly report to DADMS	acs
	Jan. 26		La Cⁱᵉ MARMEUSE to FOSSE (M.O. 10ᵗʰ R.F.) to select site for incinerators. Inspected ration dump. LESTREM. To Hqrs Corps Heavy Artillery.	acs
	Jan. 27		To VIEILLE CHAPELLE & Field Cashier. Inspected billets A Batt⁰ 126 Bᵈᵉ R.F.A. also Bombing & Lewis Gun schools. To LES LOBES. Visited LESTREM (Hqʳ) area	acs
	Jan. 28		To La Cⁱᵉ MARMEUSE & L'EPINETTE. To Ordnance. To LA GORGUE to see O.C. 52 Div. San. Sec¹.	acs

A 5834 Wt. W 4973/M687 750,000 8/16 D. D. & L. Ltd. Forms/C.2118/13.

WAR DIARY
or
INTELLIGENCE SUMMARY.

(Erase heading not required.)

Army Form C. 2118.

SANITARY SECTION.

1ST LONDON .... SANITARY CO

Place	Date	Hour	Summary of Events and Information	Remarks and references to Appendices
LESTREM	29.1.17		Organisation of School for water duty men — Demonstration of sterilisation & clarification.	aan
do	30.1.17		Lecture to W.D. men. Sent car to Divl. Gas School. Spraying infected billets at Fosse	acs
do	31.1.17		To LOCON. To MERVILLE to Mobile Lab. Received notice of movement of Division.	aee
				W Beaver Lt RAMC

Confidential

War Diary

— of —

Sanitary Section, 37th Division.

From: February 1st 1917. To: February 28th 1917.

(Volume XIX)

COMMITTEE FOR THE
MEDICAL HISTORY OF THE WAR
Date 4 — APR. 1917

Army Form C. 2118.

WAR DIARY
or
INTELLIGENCE SUMMARY.
(Erase heading not required.)

37 SANITARY SECTION.
1ST ... ARMY CO...

Instructions regarding War Diaries and Intelligence Summaries are contained in F.S. Regs., Part II. and the Staff Manual respectively. Title pages will be prepared in manuscript.

Place	Date	Hour	Summary of Events and Information	Remarks and references to Appendices
LESTREM	Feb 1		To LE TOURET, LACOUTURE, VIEILLE CHAPELLE, LES & MAISONS re arrangements for moving Sant Town Mayor VIEILLE CHAPELLE & BRAQUET. Staff Capt 112th Bde. Lecture to Water Duty men.	acs
"	Feb 2		To Div. Area to inspect whole of area on evacuation. Paid men at VIEILLE CHAPELLE & at Hqrs.	acs
"	Feb 3		To LA GORGUE with DADMS to meet O.C. 58th San Sectn. To BOUT DEVILLE to inspect area. To LOCON. Evacuation report not submitted.	acs
"	Feb 4		To BETHUNE to visit billettes. there. Visit inspection of Section & attached men.	acs
"	Feb 5		To MERVILLE to No 3 Mobile Lab. The Scabies Hospital. To CALONNE (50:7A) Conference at ADMS office	acs
"	Feb 6		To BETHUNE with clothing for men. To LA GORGUE to arrange details of handing over.	acs
"	Feb 7		To ESSARS. Inspected 10th Yd. with CO 2M.O. To VIEILLE CHAPELLE re Sanitary Sanitation	acs
"	Feb 8		To LOCON to visit baths there W.M.A. DMS to BRUAY & BRAQUEMONT to meet D.D.M.S. 1st Corps. & ADMS 24th Div.	acs
"	Feb 9		To NŒUX LES MINES. Visited whole area to be taken over with 24th Div San Off.	acs
"	Feb 10		To FOSSE & VIEILLE CHAPELLE on evacuation by 112th Bde. To PARADIS & PACAUT	acs
"	Feb 11		Hqrs (Lieut Rodell)	acs
"	Feb 12		Visited by 58th Div San Off re taking over our work. Off. at Hqrs (Lieut Rodell).	acs
"	Feb 13		March to NŒUX-LES-MINES and BRAQUEMONT	acb

A5834 Wt. W4973/M687 750,000 8/16 D.D.&L. Ltd. Forms/C.2118/13.

Army Form C. 2118.

WAR DIARY
or
INTELLIGENCE SUMMARY.
(Erase heading not required.)

Army Form C. 2118.

Instructions regarding War Diaries and Intelligence Summaries are contained in F. S. Regs., Part II. and the Staff Manual respectively. Title pages will be prepared in manuscript.

37 SANITARY SECTION.
1ST [ ] SANITARY CO

Place	Date	Hour	Summary of Events and Information	Remarks and references to Appendices
BRAQUEMONT	Feb 14		All A.S.M.	a/c
"	Feb 15		To LES BREBIS to workshop to establish there to field Cashier	a/c
"	Feb 16		To PHILOSOPHE. MAZINGARBE. TLES BREBIS Arranged trial sanitation of BRAQUEMONT	a/c
"	Feb 17		To PHILOSOPHE. Inspected Town Sanitation with Town Major – also MAZINGARBE. Inspected	a/c
			PETIT-SAENS area	
"	Feb 18		To PHILOSOPHE to arrange man re cases of cerebro-spinal fever	a/c
"	Feb 19		To LES BREBIS. Inspected A&B Co's & E Lines with M O. Lecture to Regt Officers & M O's	a/c
"	Feb 20		Arranged billeting — also billeting of water duty men. Commenced with Classes to LES BREBIS	a/c
			to give demonstration of sanitary appliances to Regt Officers & M Os. Lecture to sanitary school	
"	Feb 21		Visited BRAQUEMONT area. 2nd To Town Major. To O C 122, 123, Bde R.F.A. Interviewed CRE Reads RE	a/c
"	Feb 22		To MAZINGARBE. 1st to York Regt Squadron of Hussars & 4th Middlesex. To 124, 6th B Batt wagon line	a/c
"	Feb 23		To LES BREBIS to workshop France. To HOUCHIN to M O DAC Inspection Baths. Div Baths fitted up	a/c
"	Feb 24		To MAZINGARBE & MAROC Inspected 152 R E & 6 Bedfords. Material smokcules workshop	a/c
			obstructed, removing obstruction repaired. To PETIT SAEN'S	
"	Feb 25		To workshop. Lines of 8th Lincolns Transport Sans report to DADMS. Conference at ADMS Office	a/c
"	Feb 26		To PHILOSOPHE & QUALITY STREET — Battery position's Billets. Arranging details of move	a/c
"	Feb 27		To NOEUX-LES-MINES to field Cashier Took sample water at PHILOSOPHE	a/c
			To BETHUNE to O C 5/26 Div Sant Sect. re having over Noeux area with O.C.	
			6 Div Sant Sect. To BARLIN to No 2 Mobile Lab	
	Feb 28		To Town Major. Camp Commandant BRAQUEMONT. To Q Office & APM. Inspected D 123, A 108 & A 123	a/c
			Artillery Wagon Lines	

A5834 Wt. W4973/M687 730,000 8/16 D. D. & L. Ltd. Forms/C.2118/13.

37

140/2043

Vol 20.

M

Confidential

War Diary

— of —

37th Sanitary Section, 37th Division

From: March 1st 1917 To: March 31st 1917

(Volume XX)

COMMITTEE FOR THE
MEDICAL HISTORY OF THE WAR
Date 11 MAY 1917

O.C. Sanitary Section
37th Division

SANITARY SECTION
37th DIVISION
No.............
Date 2.4.17

WAR DIARY
or
INTELLIGENCE SUMMARY.

(Erase heading not required.)

Army Form C. 2118.

Instructions regarding War Diaries and Intelligence Summaries are contained in F. S. Regs., Part II. and the Staff Manual respectively. Title pages will be prepared in manuscript.

Place	Date	Hour	Summary of Events and Information	Remarks and references to Appendices
BRAQUEMONT	Mar 1/17		Paid men in outside Squad. Medical exam'd men for Classification	203
	Mar 2		Inspected evacuated area, PETIT-SAENS, LES BREBIS, MAZINGARBE. Reported erection of Horsfall incinerator	203
	Mar 3		Arranged removal sanitary officers by ADMS instruction. Men returned from LES BREBIS	203
NORRENT FONTES	Mar 4		Marched to NORRENT FONTES	203
	Mar 5		To No 6 Mobile Lab LILLERS. Inspected area of 13 RB at FONTES.	203
	Mar 6		Inspected 13 KRR at FONTES. D.H.Q area at NORRENT FONTES. Arranged water supply at MAZINGHAM	203
	Mar 7		To AUCHY-LES-BOIS. WESTREHEM & LAIRES. To ROMBLY. Advance party sent to ROELLECOURT.	203
	Mar 8		To MAZINGHAM, ST HILAIRE & BOURECQ	203
ROELLECOURT	Mar 9		Rode to ROELLECOURT. Men proceeded by lorry	208
	Mar 10		To HESDIN	208
	Mar 11		To 3rd Army School of Sanitation at ST POL. To DAC. To 124 Bde RFA at ST MICHEL	208
	Mar 12		To ESTREE WAMIN, REBREUVIETTE, HOUVIN & MONCHEAUX with ADMS. To Baths at ST MICHEL	208
	Mar 13		To 6th Bn Bedfords. Bt Lance. To 112 Bde Hqrs. Commenced Russian steam bath at ST MICHEL	209
	Mar 14		Inspected DHQ. with D.ADMS. Visited water source ST MICHEL with Adjutant RE. To HOUVIN	203
	Mar 15		To Supply Column, FREVENT. Reported on water supply LA BELLE EPINETTE to AA ADMG	203
			To 13 RF at BURNEVILLE	203
	Mar 16		To Hqrs 63, 111 & 112 Bde. To ST MICHEL. Demonstration to water duty class	203
	Mar 17		To O.C. 17th Corps Laundry. To No 2 C.Y. Divisional Train. Tested water supplies FOUFFLIN RICAMETZ.	210

Army Form C. 2118.

WAR DIARY
or
INTELLIGENCE SUMMARY.
(Erase heading not required.)

Instructions regarding War Diaries and Intelligence Summaries are contained in F.S. Regs., Part II. and the Staff Manual respectively. Title pages will be prepared in manuscript.

Place	Date	Hour	Summary of Events and Information	Remarks and references to Appendices
ROELLECOURT	Mar.18		Inspected HQ with D.A.D.M.S. To NOYELLE VION for conference with D.D.M.S. Corps	
	Mar.19		To St POL. No 6 Mobile Lab. Inspected 124 Bde R.F.A. & reported to A.D.M.S. To BUNEVILLE with material for 13 R.F., 9 Div. School Water Co. 49 F.A. Force pump at St MICHEL, ? at ROELLECOURT	
	Mar.20		Visited baths 9/10th R.F. at BUNEVILLE. Inspected 11th Div. arrived at CANETTEMONT, Water supply at LA BELLE EPINE	
	Mar.21		To ROCOURT. To Mob. Vet. Sect. To Russian steam baths at FOUFFLIN-RICAMETZ. Sent Corp to SAVY. To No 6. Mobile Lab.	
	Mar.22		Disinfection of billets at ROELLECOURT. To BUNEVILLE. MONCHEAUX & HOUVIN with A.D.M.S. Sent phouche No 6th Bedfords by lorry	
	Mar.23		To MONCHEAUX to demonstrate Foden Thread disinfector to men. Inspected water supplies at REBREUVIETTE. Visited 4th Middlesex 9/11th M.G. Co. To Corps Laundry, PREVENT. Instruction in Russian case to men of Section. To MAISNIL. St POL. & TERNAS to make plans of villages.	
	Mar.24		HQ cafe with D.A.D.M.S. To CRE'Q'. To LA BELLE EPINE water station & BUNEVILLE	
	Mar.25		W.M. A.D.M.S. to HOUVIN. To St MICHEL Mob. Lab. St POL.	
	Mar.26		To 2nd Somersets at MONTS-in-TERNOIS. 9/12th M.G.Cy	
	Mar.27		Rode to TERNAS & LIGNY-St FLOCHEL. To HOUVIN, MAGNICOURT, GOUY. Inspected 63 M.G.Cy	
	Mar.28		To LIGNEREUIL to arrange billeting stuff for SGs Yd	
	Mar.30		Paid men of Section. Arranged details of move with D.D.M.S. 5th Corps	
	Mar.31		Sect. station to LIGNEREUIL	

O.O Beasley
Lt RAMC

www.ingramcontent.com/pod-product-compliance
Lightning Source LLC
Chambersburg PA
CBHW081542160426
43191CB00011B/1815